Developing
Literacy
Skills

USING POETRY

KEY STAGE 2 Y5–6
P6–7

FRANCES MACKAY

HOPSCOTCH
EDUCATIONAL PUBLISHING

Contents

Published by Hopscotch Educational Publishing Company Ltd, 29 Waterloo Place, Leamington Spa CV32 5LA 01926 744227

© 1999 Hopscotch Educational Publishing

Written by Frances Mackay
Foreword by Wes Magee
Series design by Blade Communications
Illustrated by Jane Bottomley
Cover illustration by Susan Hutchison
Printed by Clintplan, Southam

Frances Mackay hereby asserts her moral right to be identified as the author of this work in accordance with the Copyright, Designs and Patents Act, 1988.

ISBN 1-902239-14-8

◆ ABOUT THE SERIES ◆

Developing Literacy Skills is a series of books aimed at developing key literacy skills using stories, non-fiction, poetry and rhyme, spelling and grammar, from Key Stage 1 (P1–3) through to Key Stage 2 (P4–7).

The series offers a structured approach which provides detailed lesson plans to teach specific literacy skills. A unique feature of the series is the provision of differentiated photocopiable activities aimed at considerably reducing teacher preparation time. Suggestions for using the photocopiable pages as a stimulus for further work in the classroom are provided to ensure maximum use of this resource.

◆ ABOUT THIS BOOK ◆

This book is for teachers of children at Key Stage 2 Y5–6 and Scottish levels P6–7. It aims to:

+ develop children's literacy skills through exposure to and experience of a wide range of stimulating poetry with supporting differentiated activities which are both diversified and challenging;
+ support teachers by providing practical teaching methods based on whole-class, group, paired and individual teaching;
+ encourage enjoyment and curiosity as well as developing skills of interpretation and response.

◆ CHAPTER CONTENT ◆

◆ Overall aims

These outline the aims for both lessons set out in each chapter.

◆ Featured poems

This lists the poems that are used in the lessons together with the page number on which a photocopiable version of the poem can be found.

◆ Intended learning

This sets out the specific aims for each individual lesson within the chapter.

◆ Starting point

This provides ideas for introducing the activity and may include key questions to ask the children.

◆ Group activities

This explains the task(s) the children will carry out in the lesson without supporting photocopiable activities.

◆ Using the differentiated activity sheets

This explains how to use each sheet as well as providing guidance on the type of child who will benefit most from each sheet.

◆ Plenary session

This suggests ideas for whole-class sessions to discuss the learning outcomes and follow-up work.

◆ Using the photocopiable sheets as a stimulus for further work

This is a useful list of further activities that can be developed from the activity sheets. These ideas maximise the use of the photocopiable pages.

◆ Other ideas for using...

This contains other ideas for developing the skills explored in each chapter. The ideas will have completely different learning intentions from the featured lessons and provide a range of alternatives.

USING THE POETRY ANTHOLOGY

For shared reading, the poems on these pages could be enlarged by hand or on the photocopier. Alternatively each child or pair could have their own photocopy.

Wes Magee, a well-known poet who provides popular in-school sessions on teaching poetry, explains the level of poetry and related activities that children should be addressing at this age. He also gives several examples of different types of poetry which will prove a useful introduction to a topic sometimes seen as 'difficult to do' with primary school children.

For the purposes of children in Years 5 and 6, poetry study is expected to expand and intensify.

There will, of course, be teachers who are wary of and uncertain how to handle such literature simply because of the public image of much poetry. It is all too often seen as old-fashioned, concerned with matters of the heart and just plain difficult to read and understand. The National Literacy Strategy attempts to soothe such fears by taking a very practical line where poetry is concerned. That's no bad thing!

There is a requirement to read poems by 'significant children's writers'. That means poetry books need to be available in classrooms and the school library. I would suggest a mix of poets from the past (like Walter de la Mare, Eleanor Farjeon,

Robert Louis Stevenson, Christina Rossetti) and living poets whose work is widely published and therefore available, such as Charles Causley, Roger McGough, Gareth Owen, Judith Nicholls, Allan Ahlberg and the late Ted Hughes. One cannot over-emphasise the necessity of having poetry book resources in plentiful supply.

◆ *Shape poems*

By this age children are well aware that poems come in all shapes and sizes … and visual shape on the page is a crucial aspect of the poet's art. Shape poems, calligrams and concrete poetry are a specialised area of poetry.

Shape poems often seem like 'proper' poems (or verses) presented in a way which incorporates the subject matter. Thus 'Climb the Mountain' (see below) is, in effect, a four-line rhymed verse but it is presented in a mountain shape.

Shape poems have become increasingly popular in recent years and appear to be something new and innovative. It comes as something of a surprise to learn that George Herbert (1593–1633) wrote shape poems, as did Lewis Carroll.

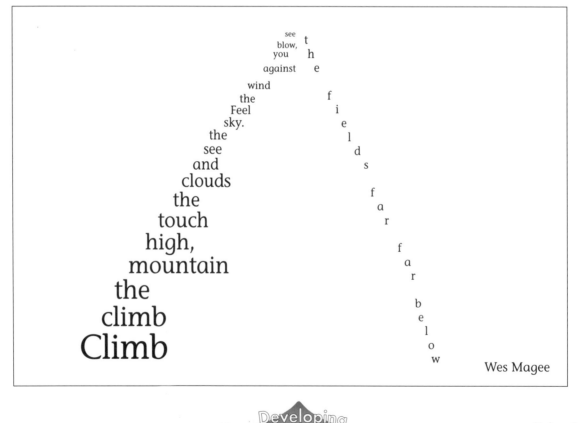

Wes Magee

Narrative and classic poems

Narrative poems and classic poems can be one and the same, such as Longfellow's 'Hiawatha', Browning's 'The Pied Piper of Hamelin', Noyes 'The Highwayman' and Robert Southey's 'The Cataract of Lodore'. Shorter classic poems are those that have resisted the ravages of time and, despite incorporating out-moded language, still retain their power to thrill the reader. Examples are Blake's 'The Tyger' and Coleridge's 'The Raven'.

Longer narrative poems have come back into vogue and Allan Ahlberg's collection of five very long and linguistically exciting poems, 'The Mighty Slide', gives ample evidence that the form is still alive and kicking. Ahlberg's 'Heard it in the playground' is a lengthy tour-de-force built up from chants, shouts, cat-calls and protests overheard at school playtime.

Shorter poems

Shorter poems can include limericks, tanka, cinquain, clerihews, haiku, kennings, sonnets, triolets and riddles. There are more! Children, and teachers, can be forgiven for feeling confused when facing such a plethora of poetry. It is best, I feel, not only to read some of these poetic forms but also to try to write similar poems, using the rules of the structures as guidelines.

Reading, for example, a cinquain is easily achieved (there are few words!) and it can seem a mite brief! Once examined it is quickly seen that the poem is based (like a haiku) on counting syllables. There is a pleasing mathematical progression about the lines.

Five lines (hence cinquain…)
Line 1 – 2 syllables.
Line 2 – 4 syllables.
Line 3 – 6 syllables.
Line 4 – 8 syllables.
Line 5 – 2 syllables.

No rhyme. The writer of such a poem must make a complete statement (or word picture) within the syllabic limitations. Children can try writing their own.

All such named poetic forms have rules. Poetry often has a mathematical basis (the numbers of lines per verse; the number of syllables per line; the number of beats per line) and as such is closely related to song.

The language of poetry

The quality use of language is an essential ingredient of poetry…

'In the forests of the night…'

'Her book a churchyard tomb…'

'it's always ourselves we find in the sea…'

'the moon was a ghostly galleon…'

It can be called heightened language or expressive language, but whatever the name the effect is to grab the reader's attention. Once read, once learned, such language can swim up to the mind's surface years and years later. It is one of life's richnesses.

Figurative language in poems adds colour and character. For example,

'This one (a headteacher) paces up and down like a caged tigress'.

and

'woodlice trundling like army tanks to the front line of some forgotten war'.

For a few poets such language falls onto the page in an inspirational manner: for most it's a matter of rewriting (drafting) again and again until the poem emerges as the best possible words in the best possible order. Children merely see the finished, crafted and polished product in the book. They rarely see the mass of work sheets (some poets draft poems twenty or thirty times) that lead to the finished poem.

Using Poetry
KS2: Y5–6/P6–7

Developing
literacy
Skills

© Hopscotch Educational Publishing

5

✦ Rhyme

As we have seen in earlier books, rhyme continues to play its part in poetry. It can be simple, as in the verse...

*'Now the days
grow short and blear.
Harvest's over.
Winter's here'.*

There we see a straight-forward a/b/c/b/ rhyme pattern. But what is one to make of the following verse?

*'Salty tears splashed down
and soaked into my book's page.
Sobs heaved in my chest.
Teacher peered over her half-specs
and said quietly, "Ben, come here."
I stood at her desk, crying. At my age!
I felt like an idiot, a clown'.*

Even when read aloud the rhyme scheme isn't easily discernible, but it **is** there. a/b/c/c/d/b/a. 'Down' (first line) is rhymed with 'clown' (last line) and it comes as an aural surprise to the reader when it eventually arrives.

Other poems make use of double syllable rhymes (like splutter/gutter), triple syllable rhymes (like scurrying/hurrying), and even multi-syllable rhymes (like excavator/rodent-baiter/buffet waiter). Internal rhyme crops up...

*'Small feet were pattering, wooden shoes
clattering,
Little hands clapping and little tongues
chattering'.*

Like the use of rhyme, assonance is a crafting tool in the poet's hands. It is a 'sound' effect achieved by repeating and rhyming vowel sounds... loud crowd, a beast feast.

✦ Finding poems

Where can children find examples of poems? In either solo collections (a book of poems by one poet) or in anthologies. Publishers are always wary of putting out solo collections (the profit motive) but even so a number of poets do feature on the market. Books by the likes of Brian Patten, Roger McGough, Jackie Kay, Irene Rawnsley, Benjamin Zephaniah and Kit Wright appear with some regularity.

Anthologies, though, are the publishers' first love. these days anthologies are mostly theme based. Some have very narrow themes (anthologies about the sea, or space, or school) whereas other compilations cast a wider net... poems about friendship, or 'green' issues, or – simply – rhyming poems.

Most schools now have a varied selection of anthologies available for children. Some books will be virtual antiques (like *The Book of a Thousand Poems*) and tend to contain a mere scattering of line drawings. Modern compilations often feature living poets (who deal with contemporary matters) and are vibrantly illustrated in full colour.

Anthologies come in all shapes and sizes; they can be 'big books', slim, bulky, paperback or in hard covers. Teachers need to give thought about:
a) where poetry books are kept/stored (library room? classroom? foyer shelf?), and
b) how children can gain access (a borrowing system? free usage?).

Thereafter teachers need to teach children how to use a contents list, an index of poets and/or first lines, and also learn something about particular poets so that they actually 'come alive' as people.

✦ A performance

Choral speaking, as I remember it from my school days, was a terribly formal way of reciting. The accent was on enunciation as opposed to enjoyment of the actual poem. CS (why not rename it? Poem in Performance?) still has its place, however children will readily learn poems with an attractive rhythm (i.e. poem-raps) and they can add actions/ movements and percussion. It really is a way of getting children to read and learn long poems, and

6

Developing
literacy
Skills

to give a polished performance before other children and/or parents. Gareth Owen's 'Ping Pong' (children divided into two teams), Spike Milligan's 'On the Ning Nang Nong', and W H Auden's 'Night Mail' all cry out for group performance!

◆ A wealth of poets

Living in a multi-cultural society has brought many benefits to the poetry world. Many writers from a host of varied backgrounds have made their presence felt: James Berry, John Agard, Grace Nichols, Lemm Sissay, Shel Silverstein, Langston Hughes.... Their poems are found in numerous anthologies, and they contain fascinating variations in rhythm, verse structures and language.

Such writers add to the continuing development of poetry for the young. The poem is a living thing that alters its style and shape, its tone and 'talk' as it moves forward with changing times. Shakespeare wrote memorable, enduring poetry. Today's poets create verse against a background that would astonish the Bard.... technology, dress, lifestyle, transport.... yet both old and new poems, in their different ways, can enrich the reader. No child should miss out when it comes to opening and dipping into the nation's poetry treasure chest.

Wes Magee is a former primary school teacher and headteacher. He has been a full-time author since 1989. For information on his services for schools, telephone 01751 417633.

Acknowledgements

The author and publisher gratefully acknowledge permission to reproduce copyright material in this book.

'The Sea' © James Reeves from *The Wandering Moon and Other Poems* (Puffin Books) by James Reeves. Reprinted by permission of the James Reeves Estate.

'Charlotte's Dog' (p12, 14 lines) from *Cat Among the Pigeons* by Kit Wright (Viking Kestrel, 1987) copyright © Kit Wright, 1987. Reproduced by permission of Penguin Books Ltd.

'Superstink' by Robert Froman from *Street Poems* (McCall Publishing Co, 1971). Reprinted by permission of Katherine Froman.

'The Concrete Poem' by Noel Petty. Reprinted by permission of the author.

'The Highwayman (Part 1)' by Alfred Noyes. Reprinted by permission of John Murray (Publishers) Ltd.

'Lion Dance' by Trevor Millum from *Let's Celebrate Festival Poems*, Oxford University Press, 1989, © Trevor Millum. Reprinted by permission of the author.

'The Listeners' by Walter de la Mare from *The Complete Poems of Walter de la Mare* 1969 (USA: 1970). Reprinted by permission of The Literary Trustees of Walter de la Mare, and The Society of Authors as their representative.

'The Terns' by Spike Milligan from *The Bedside Milligan*. Reprinted by permission of Spike Milligan Productions Ltd.

'Trees are Great' and 'The Sound Collector' by Roger McGough from *PillowTalk*. Reprinted by permission of the Peters Fraser and Dunlop Group Ltd on behalf of ʰough.

'The Leader' and 'Streemin' b⁓ ⁓ ⁓ *Sky in the Pie*. Reprinted by permission ⁓ Group Ltd on behalf of Ro⁓

'Vegetarians' by Roger M⁓ Reprinted by permissi⁓ Group Ltd on behalf of Rog⁓

Every effort has been made to trace the owners of copyright of poems in this book and the publisher apologises for any inadvertent omissions. Any persons claiming copyright for any material should contact the publisher who will be happy to pay the permissions fees requested and who will amend the information in this book on any subsequent reprint.

Poems using metaphors and similes

✦ Overall aims

✦ To analyse and compare poetic styles.
✦ To explain and justify personal tastes.
✦ To explore similes and metaphors.
✦ To convey feelings, reflections or moods in a poem through careful choice of words and phrases.

✦ Featured poems (page 56)

The Sea by James Reeves
Charlotte's Dog by Kit Wright
The Eagle by Alfred, Lord Tennyson
Extract from **As You Like It** by William Shakespeare

◆ LESSON ONE ◆

✦ Intended learning

✦ To explore similes and metaphors.
✦ To write metaphors from similes or original ideas.
✦ To convey feelings, reflections or moods in a poem through careful choice of words and phrases.

✦ Starting point: Whole class

✦ Enlarge the poem 'Charlotte's Dog' by Kit Wright. Share it with the children, making sure they can see the words. Re-read the first two lines again. Ask the children to tell you what they think the dog's ears and teeth might look like. Why has the poet described the ears and teeth by comparing them with something else? Does this help us to build up an image of the dog in our mind's eye?
✦ Re-read the next two lines. What colour do the children think the dog is? What is his coat like? Why might the poet compare the dog's fur with clouds in this way? Explain that authors use comparisons like these to help us imagine what they are describing.
✦ Explain the terms 'simile' and 'metaphor' by comparing the first two verses. (Similes are

phrases that use the words 'like' or 'as' to compare something with something else. A metaphor says something **is** something else).
✦ Find other similes and metaphors in the poem. Discuss their effectiveness/appropriateness in describing the dog. Which description do the children find the most effective? Why? Why is the nose described like a ball bounced in the rain, for example? Are dog's noses wet?
✦ Prepare the children for the activity sheets by asking them to change the similes in the poem to metaphors, and vice versa. Challenge them to think of other similes and metaphors that could be used to describe the dog.

✦ Using the differentiated activity sheets

Activity sheet 1

This is for children who need more support in writing their poem. It requires them to change given similes into metaphors and to complete a verse in the poem by using words from a word box.

Activity sheet 2

This requires the children to re-write two verses by changing similes into metaphors and then to write the last verse of the poem themselves.

Activity sheet 3

This activity is for children who are able to write a poem using similes and metaphors of their own.

✦ Plenary session

Share some of the results from each group. Agree whether the lines in the poems are similes or metaphors. Discuss how the poems could be improved even further by using a thesaurus to find more appropriate/descriptive words to describe the cat.

Poems using metaphors and similes

◆ LESSON TWO ◆

✦ Intended learning

✦ To analyse and compare poetic style.
✦ To explore similes and metaphors.
✦ To explain and justify personal tastes.

✦ Starting point: Whole class

✦ Remind the children about the poem 'Charlotte's Dog' shared in Lesson One. Ask them the meanings of similes and metaphors. Tell them that they are going to share another poem today that uses metaphors.
✦ Share an enlarged version of 'The Sea' by James Reeves (page 56), making sure they can see the words. Ask them to tell you in what ways this poem differs from 'Charlotte's Dog'. Discuss the idea of comparing the sea to a dog – do they think this appropriate? Why or why not? Which parts of the poem in particular do they consider to be very effective? Why?
✦ Discuss how the poet has used words to create the effect of the sea, such as onomatopoeic words like 'clashing', 'rumbling' and 'snuffs' and how the words in the first and second verses are harder and sharper to represent the violent waves, compared with the softer sounds in the last verse.
✦ Look at the enlarged versions of both poems, side by side. What do the children notice about how the poems are set out? Compare the use of rhyme and how the sentences are set out. For example, in 'Charlotte's Dog' the sentences often run over two or three lines and even over two verses. How does this affect the way the poem should be read? Notice how both poems use some internal rhymes – does this create a special impact in the poem? (For example, in 'Charlotte's Dog', 'When he **barks** it's a **shark** of a sound that bites' creates the effect of the dog barking.)
✦ Next, ask the children to tell you which poem they prefer and why. Model how to do this by saying which one you prefer and refer to parts of the poem to emphasise your reasons. Mention in particular the effect of the use of similes and metaphors. Remind the children that it is all right

to not like a poem at all, and that sometimes we may only like certain parts of a poem – an exciting beginning perhaps or a really descriptive line.

✦ Group activities

✦ One group could write down which poem they like best and list 3-5 reasons why. Make sure they refer to parts of the poem to support their reasons.
✦ One group could compare the two poems by dividing a page into two columns and listing relevant points about poetic style, for example:

The Sea	Charlotte's Dog
Uses rhyme – no set pattern	Uses rhyme – couplets
Uses metaphors	Uses metaphors and similes
Verses different lengths	Verses same length
Dog theme	Dog theme
Uses onomatopoeia	Uses onomatopoeia

✦ One group could select their favourite line(s) containing a simile or metaphor and write down why they think this line is so effective.

✦ Plenary session

Recount the differences and similarities in poetic style between the two poems. Ask some children to say which poem they prefer and give their reasons why. Have they backed up their reasons by referring to parts of the poem? Which simile/metaphor do they prefer? Compare the reasons why. Encourage the children to find other poems that use similes and metaphors in the following weeks – you may like to begin their search by sharing 'The Eagle' and the extract from 'As You Like It" on page 56.

Using Poetry
KS2: Y5–6/P6–7

Developing
literacy
Skills

© Hopscotch Educational Publishing

9

◆ ◆ USING THE PHOTOCOPIABLE SHEETS AS A STIMULUS FOR FURTHER WORK

◆ Compare the children's tom-cat poems with other poems about cats that use metaphors or similes, such as 'The Tom-Cat' by Don Marquis (*The Puffin Book of Classic Verse*, edited by Raymond Wilson, 1997).

◆ Ask children working on the same activity sheets to share their poems and agree on a group poem that uses the 'best' lines from several children's poems.

◆ Make a class anthology of cat poems, beginning with the poems on the activity sheets.

◆ Share cat poems, such as in the book *Cat Poems* selected by Myra Cohn Livingston (1989, Oxford University Press).

◆ Write poems about other animals. Make a class anthology.

◆ Ask the children to write a story about the cat in the poem and how he came to be so scruffy and battered.

◆ Explore adjectives further by using a thesaurus to find synonyms for the describing words used. Order sets of words to identify shades of meaning.

◆ Ask the children to write a newspaper report about the cat in the poem, to accompany a 'wanted' poster. Why is the cat notorious? Why is his capture so important?

◆ Set the children a fact-finding task to find out certain things about cats – such as why their tongues are so rough or why they have whiskers.

◆ ◆ OTHER IDEAS FOR USING POEMS WITH METAPHORS AND SIMILES

◆ Ask the children to use the information in the poem to design an advertisement/poster to accompany the poem. For example, 'Charlotte's Dog' could have a drawing of the dog with lines from the poem used as labels.

◆ Compare classic with modern-day poems. Are the similes/metaphors used in classic poems still relevant today? Has the meaning of some phrases changed over time? Is the use of simile and metaphor more common in classic poems?

◆ Ask the children to write poems about people using similes to describe body parts, for example:

She's got hair like…
Eyes like…
A nose like…
A mouth like…

◆ Ask the children to describe themselves in a poem using similes, for example:

I am as tall as a house,
I am as clumsy as a clown,
I am as young as a kitten
And I am as sad as a frown.

Developing
Literacy
Skills

✦ The tom-cat ✦

✦ Re-write the first verse of this poem about a tom-cat by changing the similes into metaphors. The first one has been done for you.

Tom-cat's eyes are like stars in the sky

Tom-cat's eyes are stars in the sky

His ears are like tattered leaves

_____

His teeth are like little rose thorns

_____

And his tail's like a rolled-up sleeve

_____

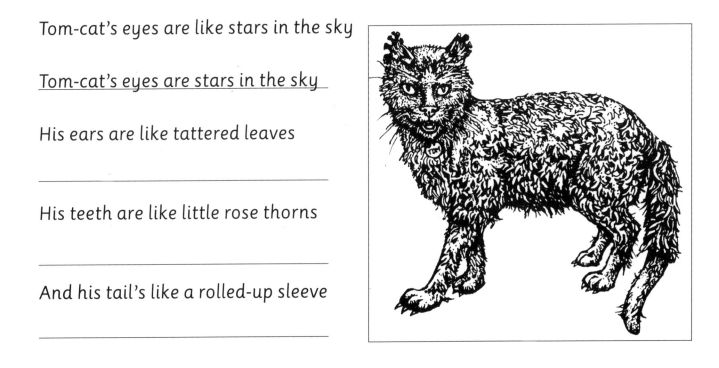

✦ Now complete the poem by using the picture, the words in the word box and a dictionary to help you. Use metaphors and similes.

Tom-cat's fur is like _____
His miaow is a _____
His claws are as sharp as _____
And his paws are _____

rumpled	hair	matted	wire-wool	messy	wool
loud siren		crying baby		warning sign	horror movie
pins	knives		needles		razor blades
padded cushions		cotton wool		tiny pads	soft slippers

◆ The tom-cat ◆

✦ Re-write the first two verses of this poem about a tom-cat by changing the similes into metaphors.

Tom-cat's eyes are like glittering diamonds   _____

His ears are like caterpillar-chewed leaves   _____

His teeth are as sharp as spiky thorns   _____

And his battered tail's like a rolled-up sleeve _____

Tom-cat's fur is like matted wire-wool   _____

His miaow is like a ghostly ghoul   _____

His claws are as long as eagle talons   _____

And his paws are like soft cotton wool   _____

✦ Now complete the poem by writing another verse of your own. Remember to use similes and metaphors. Use a dictionary to help you.

Tom-cat's _____

His _____

His _____

And _____

✦ The tom-cat ✦

✦ Use this picture to write a descriptive poem about a tom-cat. Use a metaphor or simile in each line of your poem. Try to use interesting words and phrases. The first verse has been done for you.

Tom-cat's eyes are like glittering diamonds
His teeth are like sharpened stakes
His ears are battle-worn soldiers
And his tail is a charmed snake

_____

_____

_____

_____

_____

_____

_____

_____

_____

_____

_____

13

Concrete poems

✦ Overall aims

- ✦ To read and share a range of concrete poems.
- ✦ To collect different examples of poems where form relates to meaning.
- ✦ To explain and justify personal tastes.
- ✦ To select the most appropriate words and style of presentation in writing a concrete poem.

✦ Featured poems (page 57)

Superstink by Robert Froman
The Concrete Poem by Noel Petty
A cello by Richard Lester
Butterfly by Frances Mackay

✦ LESSON ONE ✦

✦ Intended learning

- ✦ To read and share a range of concrete poems.
- ✦ To collect different examples of poems where form relates to meaning.
- ✦ To explain and justify personal tastes.

✦ Starting point: Whole class

- ✦ Tell the children that they are going to share some special poems called concrete poems and that they might be able to work out what type of poems these are after they have read 'The Concrete Poem' by Noel Petty.
- ✦ Share the poem. Can the children make suggestions as to what a concrete poem is? Explain that in concrete poems the layout of the words represents an aspect of the subject. These poems make a visual impact as well as an aural one. Refer the children to the lines:
  So that the poem's reader
  Can look as well as hear
in Noel Petty's poem, where he emphasises this.

- ✦ Go through the poem again, stopping to discuss the meaning of any unfamiliar words as well as thought provoking lines such as:
  For concrete's rather heavy
  And words are rather light.
- ✦ Ask the children to tell you what they think of the poem. Do they like the idea of poems written in the shape of what they are about? Does it enhance the poem? Why/why not?
- ✦ Explain that concrete poems can be presented in many different forms and share the other poems on page 57 to illustrate this. Which poem do the children like best? Ask them to support their opinions by referring to aspects of the particular poem. Model how to do this by saying which one you prefer, giving your reasons why.

✦ Group activities

Provide the children with a collection of poetry books that contain examples of concrete poems. They could carry out the following activities:
- ✦ Sort through the collection to find one concrete poem that they particularly like and write down a paragraph (or a list of points) saying why they like the poem and how its shape enhances the poem's meaning.
- ✦ Sort through the collection to select a concrete poem they do not like and write down a paragraph explaining why. Ask them to make some suggestions as to how they think it may be improved.

✦ Plenary session

Bring the whole class together again when the children have completed their tasks. How many poems could the children find? Ask some children to share their ideas about a poem they liked or disliked. Have they backed up their reasons by referring to the form and content of the poem? Make a class anthology of the poems found in the books. Encourage the children to add to the anthology over time.

Developing
literacy
Skills

◆ LESSON TWO ◆

◆ Intended learning

◆ To select the most appropriate words and style of presentation in writing a concrete poem.

◆ Starting point: Whole class

◆ Ask the children to remind you what a concrete poem is. Do they think these types of poems would be easier or more difficult to write than other poems? Why?

◆ Tell them that you are going to show them one way to approach the writing of a concrete poem so that they can write one themselves.

◆ Explain that the poet would first need to think of a subject he/she wanted to write about. Say that for today's purpose, the subject is going to be ice-cream! Ask the children to suggest possibilities for what the shape of a poem about ice-cream might look like. On the board, draw an ice-cream cone, ice-lolly, ice-cream sundae and other possible shapes. Select the shape most children prefer.

◆ Now explain that the poet would need to think carefully about what he/she might want to say about ice-cream. Tell the children that one way to do this is to think of lots of different words to describe ice-cream. Brainstorm lists of words about ice-cream – what it looks like, what it tastes like, flavours/colours/shapes, what it does (drip, melt) and so on.

◆ Together, agree on the opening lines for the poem by using words from the lists for inspiration. Model how to use a thesaurus to find more appropriate/descriptive words. If you think it appropriate, discuss other decisions the poet may have to make when writing the poem, such as whether or not to use rhyme. (Show the children how to make use of a rhyming dictionary to select suitable words for a rhyming poem.) Your finished class poem may look something like the one opposite.

◆ Using the differentiated activity sheets

Activity sheet 1

This activity provides the children with a lot of support by giving them a 'thesaurus' to select words from to complete a poem.

Activity sheet 2

This activity requires the children to use a thesaurus to improve the words in a given poem and then write two lines in the poem.

Activity sheet 3

This activity requires the children to use a thesaurus to improve the words in a poem and then complete several lines in each verse of the poem.

◆ Plenary session

When the children have completed their poems, discuss how many possibilities there were for filling the spaces or selecting more appropriate words. Share the ideas for finishing the verses on Activity sheets 2 and 3. Compare the different setting out of the poems. What shape did children using Activity sheet 3 use? A cloud? Lightning bolt? What problems did they encounter? Share ideas for overcoming these.

Concrete poems

USING THE PHOTOCOPIABLE SHEETS AS A STIMULUS FOR FURTHER WORK

✦ Make a display of the children's poems on a sky background. Encourage the children to find other poems about the sun, sky, clouds, storms and kites to add to the display.

✦ Ask the children to make up sound effects using musical instruments to accompany their poems, then perform them to the rest of the class.

✦ Encourage the children to write their own shape poems on subjects that interest them or on a theme that relates to the class topic.

✦ Ask the children to write a story using the poem as the beginning or ending of the story.

✦ Children using Activity sheet 2 could use their poem as part of an advertising campaign to sell kites and make up a poster and/or a jingle.

✦ Children using Activity sheets 1 and 3 could use anthologies to find other poems about the weather and make a class collection.

✦ The children could carry out some research using information books to find out more about the sun, how storms develop and how to make kites.

OTHER IDEAS FOR USING CONCRETE POEMS

✦ Challenge the children to select poems from anthologies and turn them into concrete poems by writing the poem in the shape of the subject.

✦ Ask the children to write poems and present them in a three-dimensional format, for example, a poem about a cube could have a verse on each side of a 3-D model of a cube.

✦ Have fun writing poems about different body parts. Display the poems as one large shape with arm-shaped poems for the arms, leg-shaped poems for the legs and so on.

✦ Add further dimensions to concrete poems by using calligrams where some of the words in the poem actually look like their meaning. For example:

16
© Hopscotch Educational Publishing

Developing
literacy
Skills

Using Poetry
KS2: Y5–6/P6–7

✦ Concrete poem ✦

✦ Choose words from the lists below or use words of your own
   to complete this poem about the sun.

fair	pleasing	glare	desired	helps	glows	thaws	covers
fine	lovely	light	needed	aids	heats	melts	bathes
clear	beautiful	sparkle	wanted	assists	warms	softens	washes
bright	radiant	glow	required	supports	flushes	defrosts	floods

The Sun

There up high in the _____ blue sky
You will see the _____ sun
It showers us with warmth and _____
And is _____ by everyone.

For sunlight _____ the plants to grow
It _____ us when we're cold
It _____ the freezing winter snow
And _____ the Earth in gold.

✦ Now set out the lines in a suitable shape to make a concrete poem.

◆ Concrete poem ◆

◆ Use a thesaurus to find better words to replace those underlined in
   this poem. Add a suitable last line for each verse.

My Kite

<u>Flying</u> high above my head
You will see my <u>good</u> kite
I <u>made</u> it all myself you see

_____

I used really <u>nice</u> paper
And I <u>built</u> the frame in wood
I painted it in <u>lovely</u> colours

_____

◆ Now set out the lines in a suitable shape to make a concrete poem.

◆ Concrete poem ◆

✦ Complete this poem by carrying out the following tasks:

a) Use a thesaurus to replace the underlined words with more expressive ones.

b) Complete the missing lines in each verse.

The Storm

A multitude of <u>grouping</u> clouds
Are _____
Suddenly the sky grows very <u>dark</u>
And _____

Lightning <u>streaks</u> across the sky
And _____
I'm <u>glad</u> I'm sitting safe inside
And _____

Soon the storm is <u>over</u>

_____

_____

_____

✦ Set out the lines in a suitable shape to make a concrete poem.
Use the back of this sheet if you need a larger space.

Narrative poems

✦ Overall aims

- ✦ To read and share narrative poems.
- ✦ To understand the terms 'narrative' and 'ballad'.
- ✦ To identify the typical features of ballads.
- ✦ To understand the differences between literal and figurative language.
- ✦ To use the structures of poems to write own verses.

✦ Featured poems (page 58)

The Highwayman (part 1) by Alfred Noyes

 **LESSON ONE**

✦ Intended learning

- ✦ To read and share narrative poems.
- ✦ To discuss the meaning of the terms 'narrative' and 'ballad'.
- ✦ To identify typical features of ballads.

✦ Starting point: Whole class

- ✦ Write the term 'narrative' on the board and ask the children what they think it means. Explain that narrative poems tell a story. Have they heard of well-known ones, such as 'The Canterbury Tales' by Chaucer, 'The Listeners' by Walter de la Mare or 'The Lady of Shalott' by Lord Tennyson?
- ✦ Explain that narrative poems are often ballads (songs that tell a story). Discuss and then list the typical features of ballads:
  1. It often has an abrupt beginning.
  2. The story is told through dialogue and action.
  3. The theme is often tragic.
  4. The language is often simple.
  5. Usually deals with a single episode.
  6. There is a strong dramatic effect.
  7. There is often repetition or a refrain.
- ✦ Tell the children to keep these features in mind as you share the poem with them. Share part 1. Discuss the meaning of any unknown words and the story plot. Briefly discuss what they think

might happen next. Tell them that you will share the rest of the poem with them later so they can find out if they were right!

- ✦ Go through the list of ballad features – do any of these apply to this poem? Ask the children to justify their reasons by referring to the poem. Explain that not all ballads would necessarily have all the typical features. Could we call this poem a ballad, then? (The poem is considered to be written in the ballad style.)

✦ Group activities

- ✦ Provide one group with a copy of a ballad, such as 'Bishop Hatto' by Robert Southey (*The Oxford book of Story Poems* by Michael Harrison and Christopher Stuart-Clark, 1995, Oxford University Press). Ask them to compare features they find in the poem with the list of typical features of ballads and mark any similiarities they find.
- ✦ Another group could be given a ballad and a non-narrative poem, such as 'Lone Dog' by Irene McLeod (*I like this Poem*, edited by Kaye Webb, Puffin). They decide which one is the ballad, listing their reasons.
- ✦ Another group could be given a poetry anthology that includes ballads. They skim and scan the collection to find a ballad, then list the reasons why they selected this poem.

✦ Plenary session

Share the reasons why particular poems were considered to be ballads by asking someone from each group to contribute his or her ideas. Discuss any problems they may have had in identifying a ballad. Did they enjoy reading story poems? What do they like/dislike about these poems? Remind them about some of their ideas about what might happen in the poem 'The Highwayman'. Read out Part II of the poem to see if they were right! (Or provide a copy of the full version for the children to read during the week – *The Oxford Book of Story Poems* [see above].)

◆LESSON TWO◆

◆ Intended learning

- ◆ To understand the differences between literal and figurative language.
- ◆ To use the structures of poems read to write own verses.

◆ Starting point

- ◆ Remind the children about the poem shared in Lesson One. Tell them that they will be looking in more detail at this poem today.
- ◆ Share an enlarged version of the poem (or make sure each child has a copy). Read the first verse. Discuss the poet's use of imagery in describing the wind, moon and road. How effective is this? Why do the children think the poet has described them by comparing them with something else? Does this help us to build up a picture in our minds?
- ◆ Explain that when language is used in this way it is called 'figurative'. Tell them that figurative language is language that uses figures of speech, such as metaphors, similes and alliterations. Explain each of these terms if necessary. (A simile uses the words 'like' or 'as' to compare something to something else. A metaphor says something is something else. An alliteration uses the same letter at the beginning of each word in a phrase or sentence.)
- ◆ Re-read the first verse. What figurative language is used? Are they good metaphors? Can a road look like a ribbon of moonlight, for example?
- ◆ Share the second verse. Are there examples of figurative language in this verse? Explain that when the language used describes things as they really are, it is called literal. Make sure the children understand the differences between the terms 'figurative' and 'literal' by using comparing sentences such as:
  'He hared down the street', 'He ran like a hare down the street' or 'He ran very quickly down the street'.
- ◆ Continue sharing the rest of the poem, asking the children to find literal and figurative sentences in each verse. Discuss the effectiveness of the similes

and metaphors used and how they add to the meaning of the poem. Is it useful to have a mixture of literal and figurative language throughout the poem? Would it be possible to over-use the figurative? What effect might this have?
- ◆ Tell the children that they will now be exploring the use of literal and figurative language further.

◆ Using the differentiated activity sheets

Activity sheet 1

This provides structured support. The children are required to change figurative language into literal by using the example given. They should also write some sentences using similes.

Activity sheet 2

This requires the children to use the ideas of the original poem and adapt them to produce their own verse. They should change literal into figurative language and vice versa, using the examples given.

Activity sheet 3

This is for more able children who can use similes and metaphors confidently. They should describe a character in the poem and write a whole verse in the style of the original poem.

◆ Plenary session

Bring the whole class together again when the children have completed their tasks. Share some of the work from each group. Is there agreement that the sentences produced have met the requirements? Check this by writing some of the children's sentences on the board. Ask the others to say if the language used is literal or figurative. What problems did they have in producing their own verses?

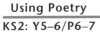

◆ ◆ USING THE PHOTOCOPIABLE SHEETS AS A STIMULUS FOR FURTHER WORK

◆ ◆ OTHER IDEAS FOR USING NARRATIVE POEMS

◆ Ask the children to write their own poem about the highwayman, landlord's daughter or ostler. Encourage them to use figurative language in the poem.

◆ Ask the children to find out about highwaymen from information books. What famous ones were there? Ask them to find out about highwaymen from other countries too, such as Ned Kelly in Australia.

◆ Ask the children to find other poems with figurative language in them. Make a class book for everyone to share them.

◆ Use the poem as a basis for a story. Ask the children to write the story of the highwayman. Why did he turn to thieving? How did he live his life? What adventures did he have?

◆ Ask the children to write about the death of the landlord's daughter as a newspaper report.

◆ Play the simile game where the children describe someone/something famous for others to guess who/what it is, for example:

> *He has ears like drain-pipes*
> *Teeth like piano keys*
> *A tail like a cotton wool ball*
> *And feet as big as flippers.*

(Answer – Bugs Bunny)

◆ Ask the children to act out a narrative poem as a play. The children could select a poem from a collection and support their choice by explaining why this poem in particular would be suitable to act out. Different groups could be responsible for different parts of the poem to share out the roles of the characters and narrator.

◆ Explore the word play and humour in narrative poems by discussing how the characters act or behave as the story progresses throughout the poem. A particularly suitable poem is: 'Get Up and Shut the Door' by Ian Serraillier (*The Kingfisher book of Children's Poetry*, selected by Michael Rosen,1985, Kingfisher).

◆ Study the characters in narratives and ask the children to write descriptions or character studies of them. The children could use lines from the poem to support their descriptions or use their imagination. 'Jabberwocky' by Lewis Carroll (*The Oxford book of Story Poems* by Michael Harrison and Christopher Stuart-Clark, 1995, Oxford University Press) would be particularly suitable.

◆ Change the story ending of narrative poems by asking the children to substitute the last verse(s) with ones of their own, using the same structure and style of the original poem. 'Mr Tom Narrow' by James Reeves (*The Oxford Book of Story Poems*) would be suitable.

◆ The children could write their own versions of the story related in a narrative poem.

◆ Challenge the children to write a playscript of a narrative poem.

22
© Hopscotch Educational Publishing

Developing
literacy
Skills

Using Poetry
KS2: Y5–6/P6–7

✦ The highwayman ✦

✦ Re-write the first verse of The Highwayman by changing the figurative language to literal language. Describe the wind, moon and road exactly as they might be, for example:

The wind <u>blew wildly among the tall</u> trees

The wind _____ trees,

The moon _____ .

The road _____ over the purple moor,

And the highwayman came riding -
    Riding – riding –
The highwayman came riding, up to the old inn-door.

✦ Now use figurative language to describe the highwayman by using similes to describe what he looks like. For example:

Use a dictionary to help you!

He wore a hat like a sail boat sailing the sea

He wore a hat like _____

_____

A shirt with lace like _____

_____

A velvet coat like _____

_____

Breeches like _____

_____

And boots like _____

_____

✦ The highwayman ✦

✦ Re-write the third verse of The Highwayman in your own words by changing the literal language to figurative language by using similes to complete the sentences. For example:

Over the cobbles he clattered like <u>a clanging knight in arms</u>

Over the cobbles he clattered like _____

To the inn with walls like _____

And shutters like _____

The sound of his tapping was like _____

And he whistled like _____

And who should be waiting there,

But the landlord's black-eyed daughter,

    Bess, the landlord's daughter,

Plaiting a dark red love-knot into her long black hair.

✦ Describe Bess in detail by changing the sentences below from literal to figurative language and vice versa. For example:

Use a dictionary to help you!

Her eyes were as black as coal (figurative)
<u>Her eyes were very black in colour</u> (literal)

Her hair was very long (literal)

_____

Her lips were like red roses in bloom (figurative)

_____

Her skin was as white as snow (figurative)

_____

She wore a long white dress (literal)

_____

And a very soft cape (literal)

_____

Developing Literacy Skills

✦ The highwayman ✦

✦ The fourth verse of The Highwayman uses figurative language to describe Tim the ostler. For example:

> 'His eyes were hollows of madness, his hair like mouldy hay'

✦ Use the picture of Tim and your imagination to complete these sentences about him. Use figurative language, such as metaphors and similes for each one.

His hair was _____

His eyes were _____

His nose was _____

His teeth were _____

His chin was _____

His ears were _____

His skin was _____

✦ Now re-write the whole verse in the same style, but using your own words. Use both literal and figurative language in your sentences.

> And dark in the dark old inn-yard a stable-wicket creaked
> Where Tim the ostler listened. His face was white and peaked.
> His eyes were hollows of madness, his hair like mouldy hay,
> But he loved the landlord's daughter,
>   The landlord's red-lipped daughter.
> Dumb as a dog he listened, and he heard the robber say-

And in the inn that was as dark as _____
Tim the ostler listened. His face _____
His eyes _____ , his hair _____
But he _____
     The _____
He _____

Poems from different cultures

Overall aims

- To read and share poems from different cultures.
- To consider the issues and attitudes featured in these poems and relate them to own experiences.
- To read, rehearse and modify performance of poetry.
- To use performance poems as models to write and produce own poetry.
- To explore onomatopoeia.

Featured poems (page 59)

Africa's Plea by Roland Tombekai Dempster
Lion Dance by Trevor Millum

◆ LESSON ONE ◆

Intended learning

- To read and share a poem from a different culture.
- To consider the issues and attitudes featured in the poem and relate them to own experiences.
- To read, rehearse and modify the performance of the poem.

Starting point: Whole class

- Use an atlas and information books to briefly discuss Africa's location, land, climate and people.
- Share 'Africa's Plea'. Before discussing the poem as a class, ask the children to turn to a partner and briefly tell them what they think the poem is about. Why has the poet needed/wanted to write this poem? Who is the 'you' mentioned in the poem?
- What is the tone of the poem? Is the poet angry/ sad/annoyed/happy? How do the children think the poem should be read out loud? Why? Why are some of the words in the poem in italics, for example? Did the poet have a reason to write it? Do people meddle and interfere in African affairs, for example? Do the children think the poet is writing about racial as well as cultural differences?

- Are the children aware that countries in Africa have been ruled by others, and that South Africa has had years of racial unrest? Are Africa's problems anything to do with us? Do they have an impact on our lives? In what ways?
- Ask the children to imagine that the poet has arranged to read the poem at a special event. How do they think he would read it? Agree on the tone of the poem. For example, how do they think the first verse might be read to express this tone? Ask for volunteers to read out the verse in the appropriate tone. Discuss the appropriate volume, facial and hand expressions and amount of pause or emphasis on particular words.
- Tell the children that they will now have a go at preparing the poem for performance.

Group activities

- Less able children could be given just one or two verses of the poem to rehearse in pairs. Provide a list of things to consider, such as: How loud or quiet? What facial expressions? How fast or slow?
- One group could rehearse the poem, dividing it into a verse each or saying the whole poem together.
- More able children could present the poem in pairs and dramatise it as if two people were arguing with each other. They say a verse each and then say the last verse together.

Plenary session

Bring the whole class together again to watch the performances from each group. Ask the children to say something positive about each one and then ask the performers themselves for ideas on how they think they could improve their performance. Use this time to remind the children about the effectiveness of appropriate expression, volume and tone.

26
© Hopscotch Educational Publishing

Developing
literacy
Skills
Using Poetry
KS2: Y5–6/P6–7

◆ LESSON TWO ◆

◆ Intended learning

◆ To use performance poems as models to write and produce own poetry.
◆ To explore onomatopoeia.

◆ Starting point: Whole class

◆ Remind the children about their performance of the poem explored in Lesson One. Tell them the poem they are now going to share is about an event that takes place in the Chinese New Year festival. Have they seen the lion dance being performed? If possible, show some pictures of people dressed in the lion costume. Explain how the people dance and move to loud clashing percussion instruments as they move along the street. Tell them that the poem uses the words 'Gong she fah chai' which are Mandarin for Happy New Year.

◆ Share the poem, 'Lion Dance'. What is happening? Why are lots of exclamation marks used at the end? How should this poem be read? What tone, volume and expressions would be appropriate? Does this change throughout the poem?

◆ How do the poem's layout and words represent the sounds of the percussion instruments and the dancers' movements? Discuss 'onomatopoeia' and find examples of it in the poem. Re-read parts of the poem together to emphasize the sounds by agreeing how words such as 'gong', 'clang' and 'clash' might be said.

◆ Brainstorm other onomatopoeic words that could be used to describe the sounds and movements in the dance. List them on the board.

◆ Model how to use the list to make up a short poem of their own about the dance. For example:

Clang, clash, bang!
Here comes the lion!
Clap, ting, wang!
Look out for the lion!
Whoosh, swish, push!
Here is the lion!
Scrape, scratch, swoosh!
There goes the lion!

◆ Tell the children that they will now be carrying out a similiar task to write and prepare their own poem for performance. They are going to describe a carnival parade, which could be for a real festival or for an imaginary purpose.

◆ Using the differentiated activity sheets

Activity sheet 1

This activity provides a lot of support for the children as it provides a selection of words to complete a simple poem.

Activity sheet 2

This activity requires the children to use the structure of the first verse of a poem to help them complete the second verse and write their own third verse.

Activity sheet 3

This activity provides little support and requires the children to write their own three verses to complete a poem.

◆ Plenary session

Bring the whole class together again when the children have completed their poems. Ask some children from each group to perform their poems. Make positive comments in relation to volume, tone and use of expression. Ask the children to suggest ways of improving their performance. Compare the words and phrases used. Did they manage to follow the rhyming patterns in the poem? What variety of onomatopoeic words were used? What problems did they have? How did they solve them?

Poems from different cultures

USING THE PHOTOCOPIABLE SHEETS AS A STIMULUS FOR FURTHER WORK

✦ The children could use anthologies to find other poems written about carnivals and festivals. They could make a class book of the poems together with information about the festivals themselves and the culture they are part of.

✦ Ask the children to turn the poems into a more dramatic performance by adding percussion instruments and 'props'.

✦ Ask the children to find other poems that use onomatopoeic words. Tell them to select the poem they like best and to say or write down why they like the poem and how the sound effects help the poem.

✦ Encourage the children to write their own poems using onomatopoeic words on subjects of their own choice.

✦ Ask the children to use information books to find out information about carnivals around the world.

✦ Use the poems as a starting point for writing a story about a carnival.

✦ Ask the children to write a newspaper report about the carnival described in the poems.

OTHER IDEAS FOR USING POEMS FROM DIFFERENT CULTURES

✦ Ask the children to write poems in response to those read. For example, they could write a poem in response to the issues presented in the poem 'Africa's Plea', writing in the same style but presenting a different viewpoint – of another African person or of a British person.

✦ Use poems that explore issues and concerns to stimulate a class or group debate about cultural differences.

✦ Explore customs and traditions by reading and sharing poems about different cultural festivals, such as in *Let's Celebrate Festival Poems*, compiled by John Foster (1989, Oxford University Press).

✦ Ask people from different cultural backgrounds to share a poem about their culture with the children.

✦ Make a display of poems from around the world, showing their location on a map, together with any relevant information books and artefacts to encourage the children to find out more.

✦ Use the poems as a stimulus to write travel brochures or posters about different countries and their cultures.

✦ Celebrate the diversity of cultural traditions in your own class or school by asking children of different cultural backgrounds to select a poem which they think best represents a custom, issue or concern relevant to them. Make a book of the poems and ask each child to write down why he or she selected the poem.

28

Developing
literacy
Skills

Using Poetry

© Hopscotch Educational Publishing

KS2: Y5–6/P6–7

✦ The carnival ✦

✦ Select words from the box below and use words of your own to complete this poem about a carnival.

bang	clang	twang	whang	crash	bash	clash	smash
clap	snap	yap	slap	tap	bong	gong	
whoosh	swoosh	hiss	swish	whish	boom	zoom	vroom

Bang, _____ , boom
The carnival's on its way
_____ , _____ , _____
We're sure to enjoy the day
Crash, _____ , _____
We can hear the band .

_____ , _____ , _____
It can be heard across the land
Swish, _____ , _____
Just listen to that beat

_____ , _____ , _____
Come and join me in the street!

✦ Now work out how to perform the poem. Work out how you will say the words. Decide if you will use any actions. How loud or soft will you say the words? Spend some time rehearsing the poem.

◆ The carnival ◆

◆ Complete this poem by finishing verse 2 and writing your own verse 3. Copy the rhyming patterns in verse 1 and make sure the first and third lines of each verse contain onomatopoeic words. Use a rhyming dictionary to help you.

Bang, clang, twang,
The carnival's on today.
Boom, vroom, zoom,
Hurry up on your way!

_____ , _____ , _____ ,
The band is coming now.
_____ , _____ , _____ ,
Come join the noisy row!

_____

_____

_____

_____

◆ Now spend some time rehearsing how you could perform the poem. Consider these things for your performance:

1 Will you use any actions to go with the poem?

2 Will some words be louder than others?

3 Where will you make pauses in the poem?

4 What tone and expression will you use?

✦ The carnival ✦

✦ You are going to write a poem with four verses about a carnival. The first verse has been done for you. Use the rhyming pattern used in verse 1 in your other verses. Describe what you might see and hear using onomatopoeic words. Use a rhyming dictionary to help you.

Bang, clang, twang,
The carnival's on today.
Boom, vroom, zoom,
Hurry up on your way!

_____

_____

_____

_____

_____

_____

_____

_____

_____

_____

_____

✦ Now spend some time rehearsing how you could perform the poem. Decide on the most appropriate tone, volume and expression to use as you say the poem.

Classic poems

◆ Overall aims

◆ To read and share classic poems by long-established authors.
◆ To express personal responses to a poem, identifying why and how the poem affects them.
◆ To contribute to shared discussions about a poem, responding to the views of others.
◆ To understand how words and expressions have changed over time.

◆ Featured poems (page 60)

The Listeners by Walter de la Mare (1873–1956)
Fidele (from *Cymbeline*) by William Shakespeare (1564–1616)

◆ Intended learning

◆ To read and share a classic poem by a long-established author.
◆ To express personal responses to a poem, identifying why and how the poem affects them.
◆ To contribute to shared discussions about a poem, responding to the views of others.

◆ Starting point: Whole class

◆ Ask the children if they have heard of Walter de la Mare. Do they know any of his poems? Tell them that his poems were written a long time ago and to keep this in mind as they share 'The Listeners'.
◆ Share the poem. What words can the children find that are not used today? Point out 'smote' and 'spake'.
◆ Discuss what is happening in the poem. Why does no-one answer the door? Can the children suggest a purpose for his visit – he said he had kept his word – what may have been his mission?
◆ Read the poem again and ask them to select a favourite part of the poem.

◆ Ask them to tell a partner briefly about their favourite part, explaining why they like it. Then share their responses as a whole class.
◆ Do the children like the poem as a whole? They should justify their opinion by commenting on how the poem makes them feel and how the poet has or has not provided interest for the reader.
◆ Tell them that they will now work in small groups to consider the poem further.

◆ Group activities

Prepare a list of 5–10 statements about the poem on a photocopied page for the children to respond to. This could include comments like:

1. The poem creates an eerie, spooky feeling because we are not sure what has happened to the people inside the house.
2. I like the beautiful words and phrases used like 'Hearkening in an air stirred and shaken'.
3. It's annoying not to be told why the traveller came to the house. I want to know what message he brought.

◆ One group could cut up the statements and sort them into two groups – those they agree with and those they do not agree with.
◆ Another group could do the same but justify their opinions by referring to the poem.
◆ Another group could use the list as a model to write their own list of statements about the poem.

◆ Plenary session

Bring the whole class together again to share each group's responses. Help them to contribute constructively to the discussion by asking them if they agree with the responses or not. Can they add anything else to the comments raised? Remind the children that we all respond differently to the things we read but that sometimes listening to the views of others can help us develop our own opinions more clearly.

◆LESSON TWO◆

◆ Intended learning

◆ To read and share a classic poem.
◆ To understand how words and expressions have changed over time.

◆ Starting point: Whole class

◆ Tell the children about William Shakespeare who wrote many plays and poems. Do they know anything about him? Do they know the titles of any of his plays? Explain that they are going to share some verses from his play *Cymbeline*. Remind them how they looked for clues in 'The Listeners' that told them the poem was written long ago. Tell them to do the same for this. Share 'Fidele', making sure they can see the words.

◆ What clues did they find that told them the work is old. Discuss words such as: 'thou', 'thy', 'art' and 'thee'. Are they still used today? Talk about the fact that these words have mostly disappeared from general use but may be retained for particular purposes, such as religious prayers.

◆ Take one verse at a time and agree the meaning. Explain more difficult words such as 'slander' and 'censure'. Do the verses still have relevance to us today – is the message still relevant even though many of the words are unfamiliar?

◆ Write the words 'hast' and 'art' on the board. Use them to explain that over the years verb endings have changed. Can the children work out what the modern-day endings would be for words such as 'goeth' (goes) and 'doth' (does), for example?

◆ Why might words change over time? Explain that there are many reasons for this and that some words fall out of use, some change their meaning and new words are invented, such as :
  – someone uses a word or phrase in a particular way and, because he/she is well known, everyone begins to use it, for example: 'loadsamoney' (first used by the comedian Harry Enfield).
  – phrases can be reduced to an acronym and then the acronym becomes a word in general use, for example: RAM (Random Access Memory).

teenage dances and fads develop their own special language and often change the meaning of words already in use, for example: 'rage' which can now mean a dance or a party rather than to mean anger, as in 'Fidele'. (*A Concise Dictionary of New Words* by Elsie Phythian and Richard Cox, 1996, Hodder & Stoughton contains information about how words have changed their meanings over time, such as 'rage'.)

◆ Tell the children that they are now going to explore words that have changed their meaning over time in more detail. Explain the meaning of the term 'traditional' before they begin.

◆ Using the differentiated activity sheets

Activity sheet 1

This activity provides structured support and requires the children to match up words to their traditional and new meanings.

Activity sheet 2

This requires children to use a dictionary to write the definitions of words in their traditional and new use.

Activity sheet 3

This activity is more challenging as it requires the children to show they understand the traditional and new meanings of words by using the words in sentences.

◆ Plenary session

Bring the whole class together again and share the meanings of the words from each group. Make a class list of the words the children listed themselves - how many were known? Encourage the children to find more words to add to the list over the coming weeks.

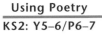

Classic poems

USING THE PHOTOCOPIABLE SHEETS AS A STIMULUS FOR FURTHER WORK

✦ Introduce the children to dictionaries of slang, phrases and etymology to explore word meanings and derivations further.

✦ Make a class dictionary of words with traditional and new meanings, beginning with those on the activity sheets. Encourage the children to add to the dictionary over time.

✦ Explore totally new words that have come into our language, such as: 'wheelie', 'whammy', 'trainers', 'nimby' (not in my back yard) and 'couch potato'. Use a dictionary of new words to find out their origins.

✦ Explore acronyms. Challenge the children to make up their own.

✦ Investigate words that have entered the English language from other languages, such as ballet, bouquet, cafe, camouflage, blitz, safari and sari.

✦ Read and share poems written in old English and try and interpret their meanings.

✦ Explore how different dialects and countries can have different words for the same thing, for example: gas (American) and petrol (English) or pumps, sand-shoes, daps and plimsolls.

OTHER IDEAS FOR USING CLASSIC POEMS

✦ Omit the last verse of a classic poem and challenge the children to write it themselves, copying the poem's structure and style.

✦ Challenge the children to prepare a poem or some verses from a poem as a playscript. Discuss how the dialect, dress and mannerisms may differ from today.

✦ Study several poems by the same poet and discuss what is special about their work. Share opinions about styles and themes used.

✦ Compare and evaluate a Shakespearean play in print and a film/television version. What are the similarities and differences? How differently are the characters and plot treated? Does seeing the story affect the children's response to it?

✦ Compare modern-day and classic poems on the same theme. How does the treatment of subject matter and the language used differ?

✦ Ask the children to write a glossary of terms to accompany a poem so that others can understand the poem more fully.

✦ Ask the children to research the period of time in which the poem was written or of which the subject was about. This will enable them to put the poem in context and to appreciate the subject matter more fully.

✦ Word meanings ✦

✦ Match each word to its two meanings. One has been done for you.

traditional meaning

| a container used for holding or serving food |
| to try to hit at something with a sweeping blow |
| a small rodent with a long tail |
| a mark left after a small piece has broken off something or a thin slice of cooked potato |
| the top of a desk |
| bad or naughty |
| a strong thick rope of hemp or wire |
| a colour like fresh grass |

mouse
green
dish
wicked
swipe
chip
desk top
cable

new meaning

| to pass a switch card through an electronic till |
| concerned with looking after the environment |
| a tiny wafer of silicon in an electronic circuit |
| a hand-held device used to control the cursor on a computer |
| a personal computer that fits on a desk top |
| a television service supplied by cable |
| a dish-shaped aerial used to receive satellite television programmes |
| very good |

✦ What other words do you know that have changed their meanings over time? Write a list of the words on the back of this sheet.

✦ Word meanings ✦

✦ Use a dictionary to write the traditional and new meanings
  of these words. The first one has been done for you.

rap _to strike against something with a sharp quick blow (traditional)_

fast talking spoken over a musical background (new)

menu _____

_____

hardware _____

_____

bottle _____

_____

cool _____

_____

green _____

_____

moonwalk _____

_____

chip _____

_____

✦ On the back of this sheet list any other
  words you know that have changed
  their meanings.

Developing
literacy
Skills

✦ Word meanings ✦

✦ Write two sentences for each of these words to show the traditional and new meanings of the words. Use a dictionary to help you. The first one has been done for you.

cowboy *The cowboy chased after the Indians. (traditional)*

     The builder was a cowboy. (new)

icon   _____

     _____

awesome _____

     _____

crucial   _____

     _____

window _____

     _____

green   _____

     _____

grey area _____

     _____

launder _____

     _____

✦ On the back of this sheet list any other words you know that have changed their meanings.

Developing
Literacy
Skills

Overall aims

+ To investigate the appeal of humorous poems.
+ To investiagte how poets play with meanings.
+ To write own limericks.
+ To share nonsense poems and investigate how meaning can be made from nonsense words.
+ To experiment with language by creating new words.

Featured poems (page 61)

The Terns by Spike Milligan
An old couple living in Gloucester – Anon
There was an old lady of Chertsey by Edward Lear
Wooden Whistle – Anon
Jabberwocky by Lewis Carroll

◆ LESSON ONE ◆

Intended learning

+ To investigate the appeal of humorous poems.
+ To investigate how poets play with meanings.
+ To write own limericks.

Starting point: Whole class

+ Ask the children if they enjoy reading funny poems. What kind do they like best? Why? Tell them that they are going to share some poems today that they may find funny.
+ Share 'The Terns'. Do they find this funny? Why? Explain that when a word like 'tern' is used to exploit a double meaning, it is called a pun. Tell them that people often use puns to make jokes and that poets can use them to make a play on words to create humour. This poem makes use of a well-known proverb as its 'punch-line'.
+ Share 'Wooden Whistle', making sure the children can see the words. How has the poet played with the words to create humour?

+ Explain that sometimes poets even make up words to create humour and to fit the rhyming pattern or structure. Share 'An old couple living in Gloucester' to illustrate this. Discuss how the poet has played with the words 'loucester', 'spacht' and 'toucester'. How effective do they think it is? What type of poem is this?
+ Explain that limericks are an old form of poetry that usually consists of five lines, rhyming a,a,b,b,a. Tell them that a well-known poet, Edward Lear, wrote a lot of these poems and that they usually began with an introduction about a person from a particular town or place. Share 'There was an old lady of Chertsey'. Have they read other limericks? Do they find them funny?
+ Model how to write a limerick by producing a class one together, perhaps about an invented character. Make sure the children understand the rhyming pattern and that they can 'cheat' when they cannot think of a word to rhyme by inventing their own words!

Group activities

+ Give less able children copies of limericks from books with some of the words blotted out. Ask them to write in the missing words.
+ Another group could be given the first two lines of a limerick as a starting point to complete it themselves.
+ Provide more able children with a collection of limericks to use as a stimulus to write their own.

Plenary session

Share some poems from each group. Did anyone manage to make up their own words to complete the rhyme? Which ones do the children find particularly funny? Why? If the child agrees, try to improve one of the limericks by working on the poem together – can more effective lines be created?

38
© Hopscotch Educational Publishing

Developing
literacy
Skills

Using Poetry
KS2: Y5–6/P6–7

◆ LESSON TWO ◆

◆ Intended learning

◆ To share a nonsense poem and investigate how sense can be made out of nonsense words.
◆ To experiment with language by creating new words.

◆ Starting point: Whole class

◆ Remind the children how poets play with word meanings and sounds. Tell them that some poets can take this idea even further and write whole poems or large parts of poems using entirely made up words! Explain that these poems are called nonsense poems and that Edward Lear wrote a lot of this type of poems.
◆ Tell them that Lewis Carroll was another writer who enjoyed doing this, especially in his books *Alice's Adventures in Wonderland* (1865) and *Through the Looking- Glass* (1872). Are the children familiar with these stories?
◆ Tell them that they are going to share a poem from his second book called *Jabberwocky*. Share the poem, making sure they can see the words.
◆ Discuss the story in the poem. Are they still able to say what happened, even though the poem contains a lot of made up or nonsense words?
◆ Ask them why they think the poet has used these words – is it to create strangeness and mystery? How might he have come up with these words? Explain that we are told how in the story *Through the Looking Glass*, when Humpty Dumpty explains to Alice that some of the words have been made up by blending words together, for example: 'slithy' from slimy and lithe, 'mimsy' from flimsy and miserable and 'mome' from far from and home. Explain that there is a special term used to describe how words have been formed from combining two or more words – portmanteau. Knowing how some of the words were created can help them to make sense of their meaning. Point out that some of the words, such as 'gyre' and 'gimble' have been made up to sound like their meaning (onomatopoeia) and are just fun to say.

◆ Re-read some of the lines of the poem – what might some of the nonsense words mean? 'Vorpal sword' and 'frumious', for example.
◆ Ask the children to make up some words of their own to replace those in the poem. Can they think up a good word to describe the Bandersnatch and the toves, for example? How did they come up with their word? Did they join words together or just make up a word they like the sound of?
◆ Explain that they will now have the opportunity to have more fun with making up words of their own!

◆ Using the differentiated activity sheets

Activity sheet 1

This provides structured support. They have to join two given words together to make one new word.

Activity sheet 2

This activity requires more ingenuity as the children have to decide which words from a given list could be joined together to form a new word. It also requires them to write a definition for each invented word.

Activity sheet 3

This requires the children to combine given root words and prefixes to other words of their own choice to create new words. They are also required to write the definitions of the invented words.

◆ Plenary session

Ask children from each group to read out their invented words. Can others guess their definition? What funny words were included in their sentences? Can others guess what the sentences mean? List some of the funnier invented words. Encourage them to add to the list over the coming weeks to sustain their interest and to encourage experimentation with language.

Humorous poems

USING THE PHOTOCOPIABLE SHEETS AS A STIMULUS FOR FURTHER WORK

◆ The children could use their invented words to create poems of their own like *Jabberwocky*.

◆ Play 'gobbledespeak'. Ask the children to write short conversations using invented words. Act them out. Can others guess the meaning?

◆ Explore prefixes, root words and suffixes. Ask the children to provide definitions of words that include known word parts.

◆ Investigate how words come into our language. Use a dictionary of new words or etymology to find out the source and development of words.

◆ Encourage the children to explore poetry anthologies to find other poems that use nonsense words. Make a class book of them.

◆ Find out how words have been created from the names of famous people. For example, nicotine (Jean Nicot), bloomers (Amelia Bloomer), hansom cab (J A Hansom), magnolia (Pierre Magnol) and watt (James Watt). Ask the children to imagine they will invent something – what new name will be coined to go with their surname?

◆ Ask the children to invent words that sound like their meaning, such as angry words, happy words, words to annoy others and so on!

OTHER IDEAS FOR USING HUMOROUS POEMS

◆ Ask the children to write clerihews – four-line poems that rhyme a,a,b,b, invented by Edmund Clerihew Bentley. They are biographical poems normally about a famous person whose name usually appears in the first line. There is often a witty comment made about the person, for example:

> *Henry VIII just couldn't decide*
> *Which wife to have at his side*
> *So he killed them off – just like that*
> *And sat around eating and getting fat!*

◆ Explore poems that contain kennings – words that describe something without using its proper name. For example:

> *Four stiff standers,*
> *Four dilly-danders,*
> *Two lookers,*
> *Two crookers*
> *And a wig-wag!*   (Traditional)

(a cow)

◆ Have fun writing humorous distychs (complete poems of two lines). For example:

> **On the Tomb of a Dentist**
> *Stranger, approach this spot with gravity,*
> *John Brown is filling his last cavity.*

◆ Ask the children to find a poem they find particularly humorous and write a paragraph explaining why they like it so much. Put the poems and writing into a book for all the class to share.

◆ Write riddles in rhyme. For example:

> *Two bodies have I;*
> *Tho' both join'd in one,*
> *The stiller I stand,*
> *The faster I run.*

(hour glass)

◆ Making up words ◆

◆ Invent some new words of your own by joining up the pairs of words below. For example:

shout and scream could make **shream** (<u>sh</u> and <u>ream</u>)

laugh and giggle could make **liggle** (<u>l</u> and <u>iggle</u>)

rabbit and kangaroo could make **rabbaroo** (<u>rabb</u> and <u>aroo</u>)

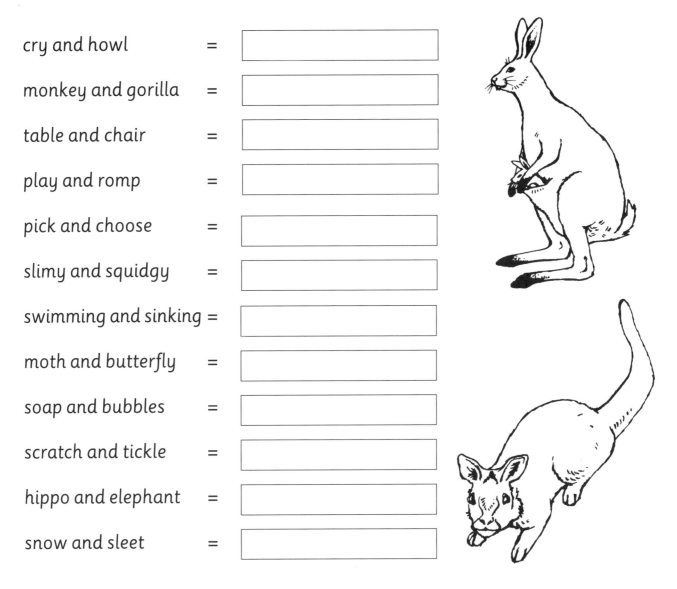

cry and howl   =

monkey and gorilla   =

table and chair   =

play and romp   =

pick and choose   =

slimy and squidgy   =

swimming and sinking   =

moth and butterfly   =

soap and bubbles   =

scratch and tickle   =

hippo and elephant   =

snow and sleet   =

◆ Now have some fun making up sentences using your made up words. Write them on the back of this sheet. For example:

The rabbaroo shreamed when he saw the mutterfly but then he liggled when he realised it was his friend.

✦ Making up words ✦

✦ Invent some words of your own by joining up two or more words from those in the box. Make up suitable definitions for each one. For example:

goat and sheep = geep – a goat with wool

laugh and giggle = liggle – to laugh and giggle at the same time

laugh	cry	sing	giggle	shout	scream	yell	smile
sheep	cat	rabbit	goat	elephant	donkey	snake	
slimy	gooey	sticky	soft	foggy	misty	cold	hot
yellow	blue	orange	green	red	white	pink	
rose	daffodil	carnation	daisy	bluebell	tulip		

✦ Write your invented words and their definitions here.

✦ Now have some fun making up some sentences using these words. Write them on the back of this sheet.

For example: The geep liggled when he saw the grink rabbphant.

Developing Literacy Skills

◆ Making up words ◆

◆ Invent some words of your own by combining words with any of the prefixes or root words in the box below. For example, if we added these prefixes and root words to the word 'home', we would get:

poli + home = polihome – a city home   poly + home = polyomes – many homes

mono + home = monome – a single home   bell + home = bellome – beautiful home

grand + home = grandome – a grand home   home + bio = hombio – home life

---

Root words and prefixes and their meanings:

poli (city)   mono (alone)   grand (great)   poly (many)   bio (life)

bell (beautiful)   cent (hundred)   medi (middle)   omni (all)

neo (new)   phil (friend)   phone (voice, speech)   soph (wise)

therm (heat)   bi (two)   ex (out)   sub (under)   pre (before)

◆ Write your invented words and their definitions here.

◆ Now have some fun making up some sentences using these words. Write them on the back of this sheet. For example:

The polihome was full of neoiders with centlegs.

(neo + spiders) (cent + legs)

Using Poetry

KS2: Y5–6/P6–7

Developing
Literacy
Skills

Photocopiable

© Hopscotch Educational Publishing

43

Poems with the same theme

◆ Overall aims

- ◆ To read, share and compare poems on the same theme.
- ◆ To comment critically on the overall impact of a poem, showing how language and themes have been developed.
- ◆ To discuss how linked poems relate to one another by theme, format and repetition.
- ◆ To write a sequence of acrostic poems linked by a theme.

◆ Featured poems (Pages 62–63)

Ten Tall Oaktrees by Richard Edwards
Trees are great by Roger McGough
Tree poems by Frances Mackay

◆ LESSON ONE ◆

◆ Intended learning

- ◆ To read, share and compare poems on the same theme.
- ◆ To comment critically on the overall impact of a poem, showing how language and themes have been developed.

◆ Starting point: Whole class

- ◆ Tell the children that they are going to share some poems about trees, written by different poets. Say that you will be asking them what they think of the poems after they have been read.
- ◆ Share 'Ten Tall Oaktrees' and 'Trees are great'. At the end of each poem ask for the children's immediate response. Did they like it? Why or why not? How did the poem make you feel? Why?
- ◆ Then encourage the children to discuss the poems more critically and in more detail by asking the following questions:
  – Is there a message for the reader about trees? What is the poet trying to tell us? Do the poems have a common message?

– How different are the poets' treatment of this message/theme? How successful do you think the poet has been in relating this message to us?
– Is repetition used? How does this impact on the poem?
– Are there references to changes over time? How is this represented?
– How does the poet use words to emphasise meaning? (For example: the use of 'boomed', 'screamed' and 'snarled' in 'Ten Tall Oaktrees'.)
– Does the poem use personification? Why do you think the poet used this? Is it used to make the reader relate more to the suggested 'feelings' of trees? How effective is this?
– Which poem creates a greater impact on you personally? Why?

◆ Group activities

- ◆ Less able children could write their comparison by answering a list of prepared questions based on those modelled in the class discussion.
- ◆ Another group could compare the poems by writing a few sentences about each under the following headings: theme/message of the poem, how the poem is set out, my favourite part and why I like it, special things about this poem, my overall impression of the poem.
- ◆ More able children could be asked to select one of the poems for inclusion into an anthology about the conservation of trees. They should write several paragraphs 'arguing' their case.

◆ Plenary session

Ask someone from each group to explain their task and to read out their writing. Use this time to praise the children's attempts to evaluate a poem critically as well as to suggest ways for improving their writing, for example how to refer to specific parts of a poem when making a comment or how to express personal judgements without being unkind to the poet!

Developing
literacy
Skills

◆LESSON TWO◆

◆ Intended learning

◆ To discuss how linked poems relate to one another by theme, format and repetition.
◆ To write a sequence of acrostic poems linked by a theme.

◆ Starting point: Whole class

◆ Remind the children about the tree poems shared in Lesson One. Tell them that they will be looking at some more poems about trees today.
◆ Share 'Tree Poems'. What do they notice about the format of these poems? Explain the term 'acrostic' and how each line of these poems begins with the letters of the names of the seasons. Tell them that acrostics do not always have the letters of the word at the beginning of each line – they can be at the end or the middle.
◆ Ask the children to tell you what else they notice that is the same in each poem. Discuss the use of repetition – how the first line of each poem begins in a similar way and how the end of each poem mentions the season to follow.
◆ Discuss the rhyming pattern in each poem (abcbdb). Explain that although these acrostics rhyme, many do not. Point out how the lines run over to complete the sentences in the poems, even though some of the last words rhyme.
◆ Ask the children to tell you what they think of the poems. Do they prefer one to another? Ask them to justify their opinions by referring to the poems.
◆ Sum up the discussion by reminding the children how these poems are linked together – they have the same theme (trees/seasons), form (acrostic, rhyming pattern) and repetition.

◆ Tell them that they are to write some linked acrostic poems of their own. Model how to do this using a short word, such as 'tree'. Show them how to use a dictionary to find words beginning with a certain letter and how to use a thesaurus to find more appropriate words. For example:

T rees are important. We
R eally should take good care.
E veryone should plant a tree to
E nsure they don't disappear!

◆ Using the differentiated activity sheets

Activity sheet 1

This activity provides a lot of support in helping the children write acrostic poems.

Activity sheet 2

This activity provides some support by providing the children with some lines of the poems and the beginning word of each line.

Activity sheet 3

This activity is for the more able as it requires them to write their own acrostics without support. If the children want to make rhyming poems, encourage them to use a rhyming dictionary.

◆ Plenary session

Ask some children from each group to share their poems. How many different variations could be made from the same beginning word or words? Discuss how the poems could be improved further by using a thesaurus to find more suitable/interesting words. Did having a set beginning (ie a letter or word) help or hinder them in writing each line? Does it encourage them to think more creatively?

Using Poetry
KS2: Y5–6/P6–7

Developing
literacy
Skills

45
© Hopscotch Educational Publishing

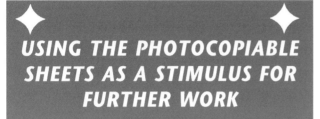

USING THE PHOTOCOPIABLE SHEETS AS A STIMULUS FOR FURTHER WORK

✦ The children could write their own acrostics to complement the current class topic.

✦ The children could carry out research using information books to find out more about the seasons. Their information and poems could then be used to make a class display.

✦ Put the poems into a class book about the seasons. Put all the winter ones together, the spring ones together and so on. Then ask the children to use poetry anthologies to find other poems about each season to add to the book.

✦ Ask the children to find other acrostics in anthologies. How many different forms can they find? Can they find poems where the letters of the word are at the end or in the middle?

✦ Challenge the children to write acrostic puzzles on specific topics. For example:

black t horn
cyp r ess
haze l
mulb e rry

✦ Extend the idea of linked poems further by asking the children to write acrostic poems for a calendar. To make the task less daunting, the children could work in groups, sharing out the months between them. The calendars could then be given as gifts.

OTHER IDEAS FOR USING POEMS WITH THE SAME THEME

✦ Encourage the children to make use of a reading journal in looking at poems on the same theme. Ask them to write notes about how they reacted personally to the poems as well as how similar/ different the poets' approaches are to the theme.

✦ Encourage the children to use skimming and scanning techniques by asking them to look for specific things in a collection of poems.

✦ Use a collection of poems on the same theme as a stimulus for the children to write their own poems on this theme. Encourage them to copy the format, style and techniques they admire in the poems and use them to their own advantage in their poems.

✦ Compare classic and modern-day poems on the same theme. Is the subject treated differently? Are the classic poems still relevant to us today? What influences appear to be apparent in the modern-day poems? For example, modern-day poems about trees may be more conservation-conscious than classic poems.

✦ Have a particular theme for the week. Share different poems on that theme every day to introduce the children to a wide variety of different styles and approaches. Encourage the children to find poems on the theme during that week to share with the class.

46
© Hopscotch Educational Publishing

Developing
literacy
Skills

Using Poetry
KS2: Y5–6/P6–7

◆ The seasons ◆

◆ Complete these acrostic poems by using words from the boxes or your own words to finish each line. Use a dictionary to help you.

The seasons

S ummer I play for many an hour
U nderneath the trees so _____
M y friends and I stay out till late
M aking the best of the _____
E very day we swim or ride always
R estless but never _____

green	big	great
tall	sunshine	
long days	tired	warmth
bored		worn out

air gusts warm and fun	
carefree multi-coloured	
very golden	
breezes bright and clear	

A utumn winds blow fresh and cool
U nlike the summer _____
T he leaves on trees begin to change
U ntil they are _____
M isty mornings begin to appear and days
N o longer seem _____

W inter days are short and dark
I hope that spring will_____
N ovember winds are bitter and sharp but
T he snow to come is _____
E veryone looks hunched and cold and
R eady to sit by warm _____

not be long	soon appear
great fun	fresh and white
evening fires	red fires

full of hope	happy and cheerful
fly and buzz	emerge from eggs
spring is here	
warmer weather has arrived	

S pring time is fresh and new
P eople look _____
R ed tulips and daffodils appear and
I nsects begin to _____
N ow the days finally lengthen and I'm
G lad that _____

Using Poetry
KS2: Y5–6/P6–7

Developing
literacy
Skills

Photocopiable   47
© Hopscotch Educational Publishing

✦ The seasons ✦

✦ Complete these acrostic poems by writing your own words in the spaces. Use a dictionary to help you.

The seasons

S ummer I play for many an hour
U tterly _____
M y friends and I stay out till late
M aking _____
E very day we _____
R eally _____

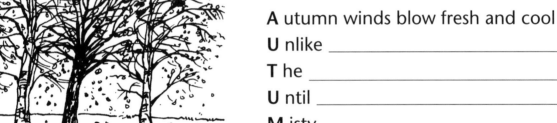

A utumn winds blow fresh and cool
U nlike _____
T he _____
U ntil _____
M isty _____
N o _____

W inter days are short and dark
I _____
N ovember _____
T he _____
E veryone _____
R eady _____

S pring time is fresh and new
P eople _____
R ed _____
I nsects _____
N ow _____
G lad _____

◆ The seasons ◆

◆ Write your own acrostic poems for each season. Decide whether the poems will rhyme or not. Use interesting words and phrases. Use a dictionary and thesaurus to help you.

The seasons

S _____
U _____
M _____
M _____
E _____
R _____

A _____
U _____
T _____
U _____
M _____
N _____

W _____
I _____
N _____
T _____
E _____
R _____

S _____
P _____
R _____
I _____
N _____
G _____

Poet study

✦ Overall aims

✦ To describe and evaluate the work of a poet.
✦ To explain and justify personal tastes.
✦ To compare poems, drawing out their different styles and preoccupations, their strengths and weaknesses and their different values and appeal to a reader.
✦ To annotate a poem in response to specific questions.
✦ To write a brief review of a poem.

✦ Featured poems (Page 64)

The Sound Collector, **The Leader**, **Streemin** and **Vegetarians** by Roger McGough

✦ LESSON ONE ✦

✦ Intended learning

✦ To describe and evaluate the work of a poet.
✦ To explain and justify personal tastes.
✦ To compare poems, drawing out their different styles and preoccupations, strengths and weaknesses and different values and appeal.

✦ Starting point: Whole class

✦ Provide the children with their own photocopy of the poems on page 64. Tell them that the poet is Roger McGough. Have they heard of him? Have they read some of his poems before? Tell them that he was born in 1937 in Liverpool and still writes poems today.
✦ Share the poems and ask the children which poem they like best. Encourage them to say why by referring to the poem itself.
✦ Compare the poems by asking the following:
• What are the differences in how the poems are set out? Compare the rhymed quatrains of 'The Sound Collector' with the unrhymed, conversation-style setting out of 'Vegetarians', for example.

• What message/meaning do the poems have? Is 'Vegetarians' deliberately provoking? Does the simple poem 'Streemin' have a powerful message?
• Does the poet make use of humour? Provide examples and comment on how effective this is.
• What line(s) do you find particularly good in any of the poems? Explain why.
• Do you think the poems are aimed to appeal to different people/ages? Why? Why not?
• What is especially good about one of the poems?
• Do you think that any of the poems could be improved in some way? How?
• What do you think are the strengths of this poet? What is good about all of these poems?

✦ Group activities

✦ Less able children could select the poem they like best and write some sentences saying why they like it so much.
✦ Another group could select a poem and list its strengths. For example for 'The Sound Collector', the list might include:
• Uses clearly-set-out four-line verses.
• Good use of rhyme.
• Uses very good words to describe the sounds, such as 'popping', 'crunching' and 'hissing'.
✦ More able children could select the best poem for a specific purpose, for example: a poem to be used as the starting point for a school assembly. The children should write down why they chose this poem in particular and how they think it could be used to put across certain issues/ideas.

✦ Plenary session

Ask someone from each group to explain their task and to share their writing. Do others agree with their comments? Has the person backed up their opinions by referring to the poem? Remind the children that personal tastes are just that – personal – and that we all like different things, so everyone's responses to a poem will differ.

◆ LESSON TWO ◆

◆ Intended learning

◆ To annotate a poem in response to specific questions.
◆ To write a brief review of a poem.

◆ Starting point: Whole class

◆ Remind the children about the poems shared in Lesson One. Tell them that they will be looking at one of these poems again today as well as reading some more poems by Roger McGough.
◆ Tell them that they will be writing a review of a poem and that in order to do this they need to have considered the poem in some detail. Explain that you will be showing them how they can do this by using the poem 'The Sound Collector'.
◆ Share the poem again. Ask the children to complete the following questions and tasks by writing directly onto their copy of page 64.
  • Circle the verse you like best in the poem. Write in note form why you like it so much.
  • Underline one line from the poem that you think could be used to sum up the poem. Comment on how this line makes you feel.
  • Mark in red all those words that sound like their meaning (onomatopoeia).
  • What rhyming pattern is used in the poem? Mark in blue the words that rhyme to find out.
◆ Share the children's responses. Have the tasks helped them to understand the poem more fully? Explain that by reading and re-reading a poem we can sometimes notice things that we were not aware of on the first reading.
◆ Now ask them to read some more poems by Roger McGough and choose one to write a review for.
◆ Most schools should have poetry books by McGough such as *Sky in the Pie* (Puffin, 1985) and *You Tell Me* by Roger McGough and Michael Rosen (Puffin, 1981). Many collective works contain his poems, such as: *The Puffin Book of Twentieth-Century Children's Verse* (1991).

◆ Allow time for the children to read a selection of his poems (you may like to work over two lessons) before they complete the activity sheets.

◆ Using the differentiated activity sheets

Tell the children that the tasks they carried out in Lesson One and the writing they completed on 'The Sound Collector' will help them write their review.

Activity sheet 1

This activity provides the basis for a very simple review of a poem.

Activity sheet 2

This activity requires the children to consider a poem in more detail when writing the review.

Activity sheet 3

This activity is for more able children as it requires them to use their information about a poem to write a review in sentences. Remind them how to set out their review in paragraphs.

◆ Plenary session

Bring the class together again to share the children's work. Ask some children from each group to read out their reviews. Do others agree with their comments? Remind the children that reviews are entirely personal opinions and that we are not expected to agree with others and that we need to be tolerant of other people's views. Explain that it is possible to write a 'good' review of a poem we do not particularly like - we should look for the positive aspects (even though we may not like the poem's subject or message) as well as the negative.

Using Poetry
KS2: Y5–6/P6-7

Developing
literacy
Skills

© Hopscotch Educational Publishing

51

Poet study

USING THE PHOTOCOPIABLE SHEETS AS A STIMULUS FOR FURTHER WORK

✦ Put a copy of the poem together with the children's review sheets into a class book. Add to the book over the year and encourage the children to read each other's reviews.
Put the book in the school library at the end of the year so other children can share them.

✦ Ask the children to find out about a poet, using information books/sources. The Poetry Society may be able to assist you with background information (22 Betterton Street, London WC2H 9BU). Make up books about the poet, containing copies of his or her poems and comments about them by the children.

✦ Ask the children to perform their chosen poem to others. Concentrate on the use of volume, expression and tone in the rehearsals. Encourage the children to use appropriate props and costumes.

✦ Make sure the reviews reach a 'real' audience. Produce a termly class or school poetry newsletter that includes the poems and the reviews. Send the newsletters home or to other classes to encourage and further develop poetry awareness.

✦ Carry out a survey to find out how many other children know the poem or like this poet. Publish the results of the survey in the school newsletter or on a noticeboard.

✦ Ask the children to copy the style and form of their chosen poem and write one of their own in the same way.

✦ Challenge the children to write reviews of their own poems! How constructively critical and objective can they be?

OTHER IDEAS FOR USING POET STUDIES

✦ Have a poet of the week/month to introduce the children to a wide variety of poets and styles of poems.

✦ Ask a poet to visit the class to share their ideas on writing poetry. If possible, organise a poetry workshop with the poet.

✦ Compare the way different poets have approached the same theme/subject. Ask the children to write down which poets' style they prefer and say why.

✦ Challenge the children to become 'poet experts' by assigning them a different poet each. Ask them to find out as much information and read as many poems as possible by that poet over several weeks. Then ask the children to prepare a short talk to give to the rest of the class to talk about the poet's life and to share some of the poems. Encourage the children to use correct terminology when describing the poems or parts of poems and to try and be objective in their discussions about the poems themselves.

✦ Make a class reference chart that directs the children to the location of poems by particular poets – to include the title of the poem, the title of the book it is in and the page number. Ask the children to keep adding to the list as they find poems they like to encourage the children to share their excitement about 'newly' discovered poems!

Developing literacy Skills

Using Poetry
KS2: Y5–6/P6-7

✦ Poem review ✦

✦ Choose a poem and answer the following questions:

Title of poem _____ Poet _____

What is the poem about? _____

_____

How is the poem set out?   Does it have verses?   yes ☐   no ☐

Does it use rhyme?   yes ☐   no ☐

How many lines are in the poem? _____

Is there a message for the reader of this poem? If yes, say what you think it is.

_____

_____

Copy out a verse or part of the poem that you like best.

_____

_____

_____

_____

Now write down why you like this part of the poem so much.

_____

_____

_____

Sum up what you think of the poem. Say whether you like it or not and why.

_____

_____

_____

◆ Poem review ◆

◆ Choose a poem and answer the following questions:

Title of poem _____ Poet _____

What is the poem about? _____

_____

Is the poem:

funny ☐   sad ☐   exciting ☐   boring ☐   scary ☐ ordinary ☐?

Does the poem use rhyme?   yes ☐   no ☐

If the poem uses rhyme, what is the rhyming pattern? _____

Is the poem a special type of poem such as a haiku or a limerick?

yes ☐   no ☐

If yes, say what kind it is. _____

Copy out a line in the poem where you think the poet has made very good use of words and phrases.

_____

Say what you like about this line. _____

_____

_____

Do you like the poem?   yes ☐   no ☐

Say why or why not. _____

_____

_____

_____

Would you recommend this poem to others? Why or why not?

_____

_____

✦ Poem review ✦

✦ Select a poem and answer the following:

Title of poem_____ Poet _____

Subject of poem_____

Is the poem: humorous ☐   serious ☐   sad ☐   happy ☐

Is the poem: narrative ☐   ballad ☐   limerick ☐   haiku ☐

riddle ☐   sonnet ☐   rap ☐   tanka ☐

acrostic ☐   concrete ☐   calligram ☐   cinquain ☐

elegy ☐   sonnet ☐   clerihew ☐   other ☐

Does the poem rhyme?   yes ☐   no ☐

If the poem rhymes, what is the rhyming pattern? _____

Does the poem use any of the following?

alliteration ☐   onomatopoeia ☐   simile ☐   metaphor ☐   personification ☐

nonsense words ☐   old words and expressions ☐   word play/puns/kennings ☐

What do you especially like about the poem? _____

_____

Would you recommend this poem to someone else? Why or why not?

_____

_____

✦ Imagine you have been asked to write a review of the poem for a magazine. Use the information above to help you. Say whether you like the poem or not and why. Write down how the poet has used words and phrases to good effect. Make sure your review is interesting for others to read.

_____

_____

_____

_____

_____

Continue on the back of this sheet

The Sea

The sea is a hungry dog.
Giant and grey.
He rolls on the beach all day.
With his clashing teeth and shaggy
    jaws
Hour upon hour he gnaws
The rumbling, tumbling stones,
And "Bones, bones, bones, bones!"
The giant sea-dog moans,
Licking his greasy paws.

And when the night wind roars
And the moon rocks in the stormy
    cloud,
He bounds to his feet and snuffs and
    sniffs,
Shaking his wet sides over the cliffs,
And howls and hollos long and loud.

But on quiet days in May or June,
When even the grasses on the dune
Play no more their reedy tune,
With his head between his paws
He lies on the sandy shores,
So quiet, so quiet, he scarcely snores.

James Reeves

from *As You Like It*

All the world's a stage,
And all the men and women merely
    players:
They have their exits and their
    entrances;
And one man in his time plays many
    parts,
His acts being several ages...

William Shakespeare

The Eagle

He clasps the crag with crooked hands;
Close to the sun in lonely lands,
Ring'd with the azure world, he stands.

The wrinkled sea beneath him crawls;
He watches from his mountain walls,
And like a thunderbolt he falls.

Alfred, Lord Tennyson

Charlotte's Dog

Daniel the spaniel has ears like rugs,
Teeth like prongs of electric plugs.

His back's a thundery winter sky,
Black clouds, white clouds rumbling by.

His nose is the rubber of an old squash ball
Bounced in the rain. His tail you'd call

A chopped-off rope with a motor inside
That keeps it walloping. Red-rimmed eyed,

He whimpers like plimsolls on a wooden
    floor.
When he yawns he closes a crimson door.

When he barks it's a shark of a sound that
    bites
Through frosty mornings and icy nights.

When he sleeps he wheezes on a dozing
    lung:
Then he wakes you too with a wash of his
    tongue!

Kit Wright

Superstink

Big bus at the bus stop.

Ready to go again.

Big noise.

Big cloud of

aaaegh

shudder gasp cough gulp

stench retch stifle

sniffle wheeze

snuffle strangle choke

poison choke *#@?&%¢*

cataarrhh ghughughughu katchoo

sneeze

Robert Froman

A butterfly concrete poem spelling BUTTERFLY vertically, with lines radiating:

The butterfly is

A beautiful sight

Its wings are very pretty

I wish I could be

A lone butterfly and

Fly all over the city

BUTTERFLY

A cello

My cello big and fat
makes
the sound
of a screeching
rat. It plays F
double sharp
when I want
it to play
B flat. It
sounds like
a bad com-
position when
I play in the 4th
position. If I try
to play vibrato my
bow goes all
s - t - a - c - c -
ato
!

Richard Lester

What is a concrete poem?
It doesn't sound quite right,
For concrete's rather heavy
And words are rather light.

Let's say you write a poem –
'Ode to a concrete slab' –
A subject none too pretty,
Which many would call drab.

Perhaps you could describe it
As full of strength and grace
And muse on what high tower
Might rest upon that base.

You may contrast its texture
With wood and weathered stone
And wonder if it will some day
Be mellowed, creeper-grown.

But if you set the words out
And shape your poem, too,
To be the slab's three faces
With each face seen askew,

So that the poem's reader
Can look as well as hear,
Why then, your final poem
Is concrete – is that clear?

Noel Petty

from: The Highwayman (part 1) by Alfred Noyes

The wind was a torrent of darkness among the gusty trees,
The moon was a ghostly galleon tossed upon cloudy seas.
The road was a ribbon of moonlight over the purple moor,
And the highwayman came riding -
    Riding - riding -
The highwayman came riding, up to the old inn-door.

He'd a French cocked-hat on his forehead, a bunch of lace at his chin,
A coat of the claret velvet, and breeches of brown doe-skin.
They fitted with never a wrinkle. His boots were up to the thigh.
And he rode with a jewelled twinkle,
    His pistol butts a-twinkle,
His rapier hilt a-twinkle, under the jewelled sky.

Over the cobbles he clattered and clashed in the dark inn-yard.
He tapped with his whip on the shutters, but all was locked and barred.
He whistled a tune to the window, and who should be waiting there
But the landlord's black-eyed daughter,
    Bess, the landlord's daughter,
Plaiting a dark red love-knot into her long black hair.

And dark in the dark old inn-yard a stable-wicket creaked
Where Tim the ostler listened. His face was white and peaked.
His eyes were hollows of madness, his hair like mouldy hay,
But he loved the landlord's daughter,
    The landlord's red-lipped daughter.
Dumb as a dog he listened, and he heard the robber say-

'One kiss, my bonny sweetheart, I'm after a prize to-night,
But I shall be back with the yellow gold before the morning light;
Yet, if they press me sharply, and harry me through the day,
Then look for me by moonlight,
    Watch for me by moonlight,
I'll come to thee by moonlight, though hell should bar the way.'

He rose upright in the stirrups. He scarce could reach her hand,
But she loosened her hair i' the casement. His face burnt like a brand
As the black cascade of perfume came tumbling over his breast;
And he kissed its waves in the moonlight,
    (Oh, sweet black waves in the moonlight!)
Then he tugged at his rein in the moonlight, and galloped away to the west.

Developing
Literacy
Skills

Africa's Plea

I am not you –
but you will not
give me a chance,
will not let me be me.

'If I were you' –
but you know
I am not you,
yet you will not
let me be *me*.

You meddle, interfere
in my affairs
as if they were yours
and you were me.

You are unfair, unwise,
foolish to think
that I can be you,
talk, act
and think like you.

God made me *me*.
He made you *you*.
For God's sake
Let me be *me*.

Roland Tombekai Dempster

Lion Dance

Drum drum gong drum
gong gong cymbal gong
gong she fah chai
cymbal clang drum clash
gong she fah chai
lion saunter lion strut
gong-she gong-she
yellow body bright eye
gong she fah chai
eye wink eye flash
cymbal clang drum clash
lion coy lion cute
she-she she-she
lion lie lion sleep
fah chai fah chai
fah chai fah chai
gong she fah chai
man walk man creep
gong she fah chai
lion wake! lion leap!
gong she fah chai!
lion angry lion cross
gong-gong she-she fah-fah chai-chai
lion leap lion high
chai! chai! chai! chai!
people cower people fly
gong chai! gong chai!
lion pounce lion prance!
gong gong gong gong gong gong gong gong
gong she fah chai!
gong gong gong gong gong gong gong gong
GONG SHE LION DANCE!!
GONG SHE LION DANCE!!

Trevor Millum

Using Poetry
KS2: Y5–6/P6–7

Developing
Literacy
Skills

Photocopiable
© Hopscotch Educational Publishing

59

The Listeners

'Is there anybody there?' said the Traveller,
Knocking on the moonlit door;
And his horse in the silence champed the
    grasses
Of the forest's ferny floor:
And a bird flew up out of the turret,
Above the Traveller's head:
And he smote upon the door again a second
    time;
'Is there anybody there?' he said.
But no one descended to the Traveller;
No head from the leaf-fringed sill
Leaned over and looked into his grey eyes,
Where he stood perplexed and still.
But only a host of phantom listeners
That dwelt in the lone house then
Stood listening in the quiet of the moonlight
To that voice from the world of men:
Stood thronging the faint moonbeams on the
    dark stair,
That goes down to the empty hall,
Hearkening in an air stirred and shaken
By the lonely Traveller's call.
And he felt in his heart their strangeness,
Their stillness answering his cry,
While his horse moved, cropping the dark
    turf,
'Neath the starred and leafy sky;
For he suddenly smote upon the door, even
Louder, and lifted his head:
'Tell them I came, and no one answered,
That I kept my word,' he said.
Never the least stir made the listeners,
Though every word he spake
Fell echoing through the shadowiness of the
    still house
From the one man left awake:
Ay, they heard his foot upon the stirrup,
And the sound of iron on stone,
And how the silence surged softly backward,
When the plunging hoofs were gone.

Walter de la Mare

Fidele

Fear no more the heat o'th' sun,
    Nor the furious winter's rages.
Thou thy worldly task hast done,
    Home art gone, and ta'en thy wages.
Golden lads and girls all must,
As chimney-sweepers, come to dust.

Fear no more the frown o'th' great,
    Thou art past the tyrant's stroke.
Care no more to clothe and eat,
    To thee the reed is as the oak.
The sceptre, learning, physic, must
All follow this, and come to dust.

Fear no more the lightning flash,
    Nor th'all-dreaded thunder-stone.
Fear not slander, censure rash.
    Thou has finished joy and moan.
All lovers young, all lovers must
Consign to thee, and come to dust.

from *Cymbeline*, iv ii
William Shakespeare

60 Using Poetry
KS2: Y5–6/P6–7

Developing
Literacy
Skills

Photocopiable
© Hopscotch Educational Publishing

The Terns

Said the mother Tern
    to her baby Tern
Would you like a brother?
Said the baby Tern
    to mother Tern
Yes
One good Tern deserves another.

Spike Milligan

An old couple living in Gloucester

An old couple living in Gloucester
Had a beautiful girl but they loucester!
    She fell from a yacht
    And never the spacht
Could be found where the cold waves had
toucester.

Anon

There was an old lady of Chertsey
Who made a remarkable Curtsey
She twirled round and round
Till she sunk underground
Which distressed all the people of Chertsey

Edward Lear

Wooden Whistle

I bought   steel
a wooden   wooden
whistle,   whistle.
but it   So
wooden   I bought
whistle.   a tin
I bought   whistle.
a steel   And now
whistle,   I tin
but it   whistle!

Anon

Jabberwocky

'Twas brillig, and the slithy toves
    Did gyre and gimble in the wabe;
All mimsy were the borogoves,
    And the mome raths outgrabe.

"Beware the Jabberwock, my son!
    The jaws that bite, the claws that catch!
Beware the Jubjub bird, and shun
    The frumious Bandersnatch!"

He took his vorpal sword in hand:
    Long time the manxome foe he sought –
So rested he by the Tumtum tree,
    And stood awhile in thought.

And as in uffish thought he stood,
    The Jabberwock, with eyes of flame,
Came whiffling through the tulgey wood,
    And burbled as it came!

One, two! One two! And through and through
    The vorpal blade went snicker-snack!
He left it dead, and with its head
    He went galumphing back.

"And hast thou slain the Jabberwock!
    Come to my arms, my beamish boy!
O Frabjous day! Callooh! Callay!"
    He chortled in his joy.

'Twas brillig, and the slithy toves
    Did gyre and gimble in the wabe;
All mimsy were the borogoves
    And the mome raths outgrabe.

Lewis Carroll

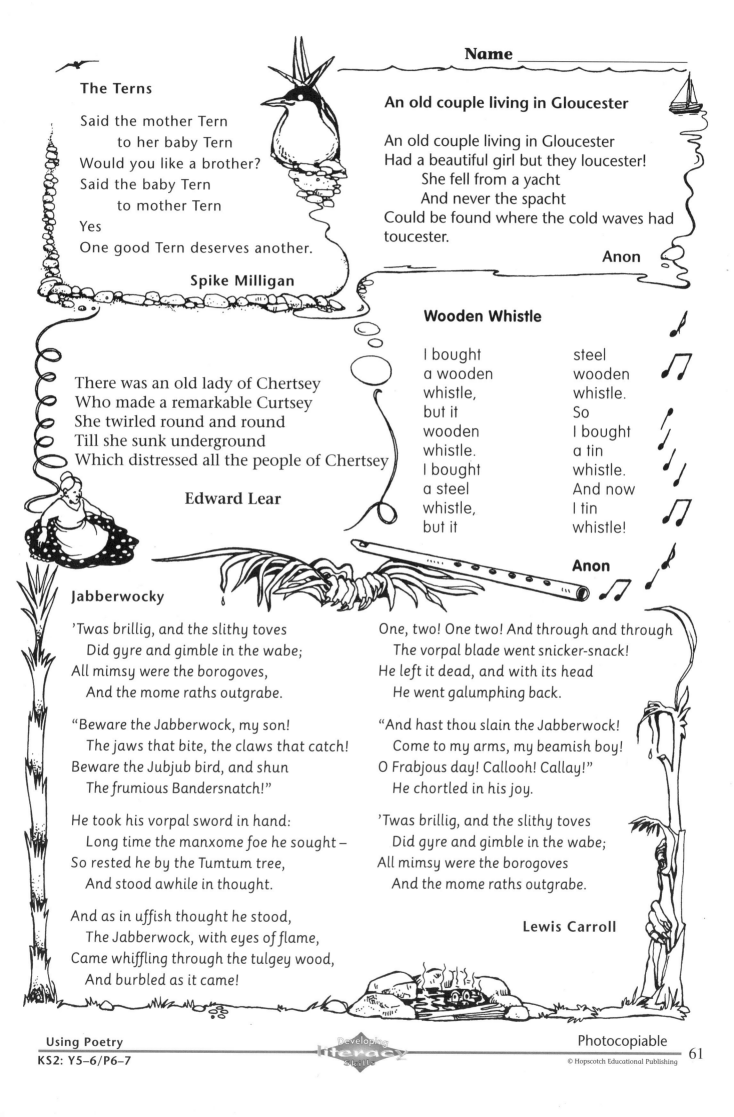

Developing
literacy
Skills

Photocopiable
© Hopscotch Educational Publishing

Ten Tall Oaktrees

Ten tall oaktrees
Standing in a line
'Warships,' cried King Henry,
Then there were nine.

Nine tall oaktrees
Growing strong and straight,
'Charcoal,' breathed the furnace,
Then there were eight.

Eight tall oaktrees
Reaching towards heaven,
'Sizzle,' spoke the lightning,
Then there were seven.

Seven tall oaktrees,
Branches, leaves and sticks,
'Firewood,' said the merchant,
Then there were six.

Six tall oaktrees
Glad to be alive,
'Barrels,' boomed the brewery,
Then there were five.

Five tall oaktrees,
Suddenly a roar,
'Gangway,' screamed the west wind,
Then there were four.

Four tall oaktrees,
Sighing like the sea,
'Floorboards,' beamed the builder,
Then there were three.

Three tall oaktrees
Groaning as trees do,
'Unsafe,' said the council,
Then there were two.

Two tall oaktrees
Spreading in the sun,
'Progress,' snarled the by-pass,
Then there was one.

One tall oaktree
Wishing it could run,
'Nuisance,' grumped the farmer,
Then there were none.

No tall oaktrees,
Search the fields in vain,
Only empty skylines
And the cold grey rain.

Richard Edwards

Trees are great

Trees are great, they just stand and wait
They don't cry when they're teased
They don't eat much and they seldom shout
Trees are easily pleased

Trees are great, they like to congregate
For meetings in the park
They dance and sway, they stay all day
And talk till well after dark

Trees are great, they accept their fate
When it's pouring down with rain
They don't wear macs, it runs off their backs
But you never hear them complain

So answer me please, if there weren't any trees
Where would naughty boys climb?
Where would lovers carve their names?
Where would little birds nest?
Where would we hang the leaves?

Roger McGough

Developing
literacy
Skills

Tree poems

S ummer trees look majestic

U nder their shiny cloaks of green.

M ighty trunks reach skywards

M aking the forest dark and serene.

E very tree stands waiting, all

R eady for autumn's clean.

A utumn trees look proud, for

U nlike their summer sameness

T heir leaves glow in many colours

U tterly magnificent now. But yes,

M ighty winds soon blow angry and

N othing can stop winter's undress.

W inter trees look sad and

I nterested in life no more, for

N ow they stand all bare and cold

T heir glorious leaves on the floor.

E ach tree now waits for Spring to

R egenerate the leaves once more.

S pring trees look fresh and clean,

P arading their bright new leaves.

R adiant, vigorous and glowing,

I nviting birds their nests to weave.

N ature now looks towards summer and

G lories in the coming reprieve.

Poems by Roger McGough

Name _____

The Sound Collector

A stranger called this morning
Dressed all in black and grey
Put every sound into a bag
And carried them away

The whistling of the kettle
The turning of the lock
The purring of the kitten
The ticking of the clock

The popping of the toaster
The crunching of the flakes
When you spread the marmalade
The scraping noise it makes

The hissing of the frying-pan
The ticking of the grill
The bubbling of the bathtub
As it starts to fill

The drumming of the raindrops
On the window-pane
When you do the washing-up
The gurgle of the drain

The crying of the baby
The squeaking of the chair
The swishing of the curtain
The creaking of the stair

A stranger called this morning
He didn't leave his name
Left us only silence
Life will never be the same.

The Leader

I wanna be the leader
I wanna be the leader
Can I be the leader?
Can I? I can?
Promise? Promise?
Yippee, I'm the leader
I'm the leader

OK what shall we do?

Streemin

im in the botom streme
wich means im not britgh
dont lik readin
cant hardly write

but all these divishns
arnt reelly fair
look at the cemtery
no streemin there

Vegetarians

Vegetarians are cruel unthinking people.
Everybody knows that a carrot screams when grated
That a peach bleeds when torn apart.
Do you believe an orange insensitive
to thumbs gouging out its flesh?
That tomatoes spill their brains
painlessly? Potatoes, skinned alive
and boiled, the soil's little lobsters.
Don't tell me it doesn't hurt
when peas are ripped from their overcoats,
the hide flayed off sprouts,
cabbage shredded, onions beheaded.

Throw in the towel and lay down the hoe.
Mow no more. Let my people go!